SCARRED, BUT NOT BROKEN

SCARRED, BUT NOT BROKEN

WHAT WAS MEANT TO BE A TELL-ALL, TURNED INTO MY TESTIMONY

L. CATRISE HARRIS

PUBLISHERS

Scarred, But Not Broken
Copyright © 2020 by L. Catrise Harris
Email: info@iamcatrise.com
Website: www.iamcatrise.com
Printed in the United States of America.
Get It Done Publishing, LLC.
4410 Stacks Road Atlanta, GA 30349
www.getitdonepublishing.com

Print ISBN: 978-1-952561-02-3
EBook ISBN: 978-1-952561-06-1

This book is memoir. It reflects the author's present recollections of
experiences over time. Some names and identifying details of people
described in this book may have been altered to protect their privacy.

ACKNOWLEDGMENTS

Before I begin, I would like to take the time out to thank God for allowing me to share my testimony. I know this book will bless and reach people across the nation with all my real-life encounters. There are so many of you out there just like me, and I can't wait to hear your testimonies.

Secondly, I would like to thank my children. Starting with my eldest, Jordan Deshon Cameron, who inspired me from day one to go after my dreams. Because of him, I wanted so much more in life, and that's where my success began.

My second child and first daughter, Jada Samarra Harris, was an eye-opener for me. Because of her, I became career-oriented, and I wanted to be able to afford nannies and high-end babysitters. Because she was my baby girl, I was so protective of her, and I didn't trust anyone with her.

My third and last child, London Taylor Harris. She

was a shock to me because I didn't expect her; however, I fell in love all over again. She was an angel sent from heaven.

I would also like to take time to thank all my family and friends who helped make this book possible. Thank you for your daily encouragement and the love you gave during my times of struggle. I promise you guys will not be disappointed.

To understand my past, you must get to know my present, which will tell you all you need to know about my future. Not what you've heard, but the truth! After reading my story and hearing it directly from me, you can officially say, "I know her."

Okay, now you must prepare yourself for what's about to take place as you read. Pour a nice glass of wine, coffee, or tea, your choice. Get your bookmark ready as you do not want to lose the page you're on. I will see you at the end!

CONTENTS

MOLESTATION

I remember being outside with my sisters enjoying a beautiful summer's day. It was the perfect weather to ride my bike. The sun was shining bright, but it wasn't blistering hot. The wind was blowing a cool breeze in my face as I pedaled as fast as I could. I was having the time of my life playing with my sisters. Then out of nowhere, I hear, "Come inside. I have some errands to run. Twinkie is going to watch you all." Twinkie was my mom's best friend's daughter.

I listened to my mom and began heading back to the house. I wasn't pedaling as fast as I could because I was disappointed that my time was cut short. I wanted to enjoy that moment as long as I could as it was no telling when my mother would be back. Twinkie's mom and my mom had been friends for twenty plus years and attended the same high school, so Twinkie was like a big sister to me. As I got closer to the house, I hopped off my bike and laid it beside the front door in hopes that my mom wouldn't be gone long. Usually, when she was leaving for a long time, she would tell my sisters and I to put our bikes in the house. My mom didn't say anything about my bike as she left, so I knew she wouldn't be gone long.

"You listen to Twinkie. Don't let me come back and hear you done showed your tail off," my mom yelled as she pulled off.

I closed the front door. I could hear the radio playing and someone clapping to the rhythm of the music in the living room. I dashed straight to the living room because it was so typical of my sisters to have fun without me, and I figured maybe they came into the house before me. As I entered the living room, I could only see Twinkie, who seemed to be enjoying dancing by herself. I began looking around for my sisters only to realize they were not inside the house. I believe they never came in and stayed outside to play, leaving me alone with Twinkie, the babysitter. What happened next is a secret I planned to take to my grave and tell no one, until now.

A commercial came on over the radio as I walked back into the living room. The commercial gave Twinkie a break from dancing, and she turned down the radio. I was looking for the remote when she plopped down onto the couch next to me. It caught me off guard because I didn't hear her walking over.

"Have you ever saw a breast before?" she asked, slightly out of breath.

As a five-year-old, I sat there, unsure of what she was asking of me. She moved in closer to me and asked, "Would you like to see my breast?"

I'm not sure of my response, or if I even responded. I do remember being scared and nervous; I just wanted my mom to be home, so all of this could stop. Twinkie could sense that I was tense because I didn't move a muscle. As she leaned in closer to me, I closed my eyes and clenched my hands right by my side. Soon after I closed my eyes, I could feel a breeze as if the presence of her warmth was no longer there. I kept my eyes closed just for a little while, hoping this was some joke that I didn't understand. When I opened my eyes, Twinkie was in front of me with snacks and juice to butter me up. After I grabbed the snack and juice out of her hand, she left the room again without a word. A sense of relief came over me. I finally found the remote behind the pillows on the couch and sat back with my feet up and began to watch television. A few minutes later, Twinkie entered the room with such an intense demeanor, I heard her footsteps this time.

She walked over in front of the television, turned it off, and stood in front of me with only a white robe on that looked just like my mom's robe. She gazed into my eyes, which made me more uncomfortable. I wasn't sure what was happening, but I did know I didn't like what was going on. My emotions quickly turned into fear. *Why is she naked in front of me? Where are my sisters? I want my mommy,*" I thought. My heart began to race, my breathing shortened, and my body became

3

cold. I had this uneasy feeling something was about to take place I didn't want to be a part of.

"All you have to do is what I tell you, and I will do the rest," she said sternly.

"What?" is all I could muster up to say as my voice shivered. The fear of the moment and the coldness of my body had frozen my vocal cords.

She didn't bother to repeat herself, and by her demeanor, neither did she care to. Before I could even finish my response, she laid down beside me on the couch with her legs propped up.

"Insert your fingers inside of me and fondle my breast at the same time," she said.

I was shaking badly but did exactly as she told me. I closed my eyes, hoping that this would all be a dream, and she would get up and leave just like she did last time and never come back. I turned my head as if I was trying to avoid a nightmare, not caring where my hands landed. I remember the moaning sounds she made. Each moan made me sicker because I realized this wasn't a dream; I was living a nightmare. The noise she made next paralyzed me into shock as she let out an intense cry as if she was relieved.

She became silent for a moment and then gathered herself. I took the silence as a sign that this horrible moment was over. I removed my hands from her body and pushed myself into a corner, not wanting to be anywhere near her. She adjusted the humongous glasses on her face, closed the robe, and stood up.

"Did you enjoy it?" she dared to ask.

I gave her a blank stare with no response. *How could she ask me such a thing? How could I enjoy what just happened?* She made me wash my hands, smelled them, then made me wash them again. Repeatedly, she had me re-wash my hands until the smell was gone from my fingers. I rubbed my hands together in that soap as hard as I could as if getting the stench off my hands would erase what happened. After my hands met her approval, she left the room. I sat quietly on the couch, dumbfounded as to what just took place. As if this event had been perfectly timed, my mom returned home.

I didn't run to the door to greet her like I usually did. Instead, I sat in silence with an emotionless look. My mother noticed I was quiet, which was rare for me since I was the talker of the family.

"Are you okay?" my mom said as she calmly looked at me.

I didn't answer her question. I just asked, "Can I go back outside to play?"

"Yes," she said.

Out of nowhere, this rush of energy came over me, and I dashed out the door quicker than you could blink. As I stepped foot outside, it didn't matter how perfect the weather was or how earlier I was having the time of my life. I felt horrible! Inside and out. I got my bike from beside the door and rode the fastest I had ever ridden. I didn't care where my sisters were. All I knew was I wanted to be alone.

I rode my bike behind an apartment building and

just cried. I felt disgusted. *"What just happen to me? What did I do to deserve this?"* were some of the questions I began asking myself. I stayed there for quite some time until the sun started setting, and I knew my mom and sisters would be looking for me. I got back on my bike and rode home slowly, hoping the "babysitter" had already left.

I got home, and she was gone. The rest of the day, I kept silent. I wanted to be alone to process what happened, but honestly, I wasn't sure. I tried not to talk, but it was the smallest and most innocent questions one of my sisters asked that broke me. I'm not even sure what she asked, but I mustered up the loudest and boldest, "What?!" I could find. My response was if I took what happened to me out on her, and I did. I could see a glare in her eyes as tears begin to form. I couldn't control myself any longer and charged at her. The feeling of rage came over me and caused me to lash out not only at my sister but at everyone. My mom rushed to pull me off her. I can't recall what happened afterward because I became consumed with rage.

Little did I know that day was just the beginning. The incident between Twinkie and I caused me to become heartless. I couldn't understand how one human being do that to another. The strange thing about it all is that even though I claimed to be heartless, with each moment of rage and anger, I felt pain strike in my heart.

Not only did my heart change, but I also started to

shower a lot more. I always felt dirty and unclean, no matter how much I bathed. Once I was done with my bath each night, I would crawl in my bed, look out the window, and cry myself to sleep. No one knew. All I could do was think of how violated I felt. *What would happen if I told? How many other children had she done this to?* I remained silent.

Over time, I became known as the "bad child," constantly getting into it with my sisters as a result of my rage and anger issues. I felt if I told anyone what happened to me, no one would believe me, so I acted out. Because of the incident, I no longer felt like a little girl; instead, I felt like something had awakened in me. I started to dress differently and cared more about my appearance. I wanted to wear dresses and lip gloss. I can't recall why; I just knew I felt more like a woman than a child.

Over the years, each time I saw Twinkie's face, heard her speak, or even the mention of her name, it reminded me of the terrible incident and sent me back into fear. I felt as if she had the upper hand. I stayed as far away from her as I could. I would show out or hide if I thought she was "babysitting" me again.

I often found myself ashamed and wanting to be alone. No amounts of Sunday worship services could take that feeling away. I thought it had to be a once in a lifetime thing, and there couldn't be any more "Twinkies" out there. As much as I hoped it was true, it happened again; but this time, it was with a man.

FROSTBITE AND ABUSE

*M*y family and I use to live in a red and white house off Cleveland Ave in Atlanta, Georgia. It's hard to forget that home because it was where I had a Christmas I would never forget. Christmas Eve morning, I woke up to the chirping of a bird in my windowsill. I pulled the blinds up and, to my surprise, saw beautiful snow falling from the sky. I ran through the house screaming, "It's snowing, it's snowing!" as if I were everyone's morning alarm clock. My sisters were just as excited as me to go outside to play. We burst into our mother's room, pleading with her to let us go outside. She agreed, but first, we had to do chores. It took us a few hours to do our tasks. By the time we finished, it was nearly one in the afternoon, so we ran into the kitchen to let our mother know we had completed our chores. She made us eat lunch, then gave us the okay to go outside but told us to make sure to dress in layers so we wouldn't get sick. I ran back to my room and threw on all that I could. I didn't own mittens, so I did the next best thing, I put socks on my hands. We ran past my mother in the kitchen and out the door as she shouted for us to slow down.

My sisters and I were on winter break, so we were out of school for the next two weeks. I was elated about the snow. It wasn't often it snowed in Georgia; therefore, I was going to take advantage of every opportunity to be in it. The first thing my sister and I made were snowmen. It took us some time to pile all the snow to make the body, but we enjoyed every bit of it. Once we got the shapes of our snowmen made, we ran back to the house to see if we could find some items to make the faces. My mom asked what all the commotion was about, then we explained what we were doing, and she allowed us to get some things from the kitchen to decorate our snowmen's faces.

We raced back outside as if our snowmen were going to melt away. I used a celery stick for the nose, Oreos for the eyes, and a trail of black-eyed peas to make a smile. Mr. Wonderful is what I named him. I found some twigs in the neighbor's yard to make Mr. Wonderful's arms. I was proud of what I had made. After we finished, we decided to make some snow angels. We laid down in the snow and flapped our arms and legs back and forth to create the image of the snow angel. Somehow it turned into a competition to see who could make the most snow angels. Before we could even count to see who had won, my mother called us in for dinner.

We wanted to go back out after dinner; however, my mom told us no. I finished my meal and went back to my room. Looking out my window, I admired the snow as it continued falling from the sky. Not too long afterward, I heard a knock at the door. I went running to the door, barefoot to see who was there. It was my next-door neighbor, Amanda, asking if I could come outside to play. I explained I had been out earlier, and my mom said I couldn't go back outside. Amanda looked disappointed, so I stayed on the porch and talked with her. I figured no harm could come from it; I was only on the porch.

I was so happy to have the company that I didn't realize I didn't have on socks or shoes as I placed my feet on the concrete ground full of snow. We laughed about Mr. Wonderful, and how not so wonderful he looked. We talked about what we expected to get for Christmas and how we wished Christmas break was longer. After about twenty minutes, her parents yelled, "Amanda, time for supper!" We hugged, and she walked back home. I went inside back into my room, appreciating the beautiful white flakes that brought me so much joy.

Later that evening, my feet started to itch. I didn't think much of it. I was too excited about opening one of my gifts as it was a tradition for my mom to allow us to open one of our presents on Christmas Eve. However, the itch started to intensify so rapidly scratching wasn't enough. My feet began to turn fire red and became swollen.

"Mom! Mom! Mommy, help me!" I screamed.

"Yea Queda!" she replied, not understanding the severity of my situation. Queda was the nickname my mom gave me.

"Mom, something is wrong with my feet."

I must have interrupted her from cleaning the kitchen because I heard the clinging of the silverware she placed in the drawer, and I heard her as she walked down the hallway. As she entered my room, I could see her eyes widening from what she saw. Her mouth opened wide as she gasped before she turned around and ran out of the room. She came back with a bottle of rubbing alcohol and instantly started pouring it all over my feet. It wasn't working because I continued to scream from the top of my lungs from the pain.

"Scratch it, mommy. Scratch it!" I yelled as if my life depended on it. The burning intensified. I could hear my sisters racing down the hallway to see why I was screaming.

My mother scratched with her all, but the itching did not let up. My mom's face was full of concern. She paused from scratching my feet and dashed out the room. The worry on her face made me panic. My sisters just stood silent at my door, trying to figure out exactly what was going on. A few moments later, I heard bath water running. I tried to scratch my feet as hard as I could, but that didn't help, the burning just worsened. No matter how hard or how often I scratched, nothing worked. My mom came back to help me to the bathroom. She undressed me and helped me into the warm bath to try to soothe the pain and discomfort. The bath helped, but I still itched but not as much as before. After some time, I felt like things were getting better. Since the water was getting cold, my mom figured if I rested, the itching and swelling would subside. She helped me to my room and got me ready for bed. Things seemed to be turning around; however, the itching pain came back and kept me up all night.

My feet were as red as Santa's outfit. The swelling got worse, and my feet began itching uncontrollably. My mother immediately called 911. My sisters sat on the couch as my mother paced back and forth by the front door. Upon arrival, the paramedics were amazed when they saw my feet. "Wow, this is very unusual for Georgia, but it looks like your daughter has frostbite," one of the paramedics said to my mom. "We would have to take her in for a doctor to diagnosis her to be certain."

As the paramedics carried me outside on the stretcher, I could see neighbors in their front yards looking at me, wondering what was going on? The sirens blared as they rushed me to South Fulton Medical Center. Here I was on Christmas Eve, heading to the hospital. Not what any child would have planned for Christmas.

Upon arrival at the hospital, nurses quickly ran out to get me and place me in a room. It was like something you would see on television, but it was happening to me! They put me through a few tests and x-rays before they could determine what was wrong with me. They couldn't get done with the tests quickly enough as my feet were causing me agonizing pain. One nurse frequently checked in and assured me once they got the proper diagnose, they would give me medicine for my pain.

The doctor finally came in and confirmed what the paramedics had already said. I had contracted frostbite in my feet. The nurse kept her promise and gave me medicine to help with the pain. The doctor pulled my mom to the side, away from my bed as if he didn't want me to hear, but the room was only so big. The doctor informed my mom it was a possibility they would have to amputate my feet and legs up to my knees. I was so confused as I looked into my mother's watery eyes. I had no idea what that meant. The doctors asked my mom for permission to proceed.

"No!" my mom shouted, "I need to know all of my options and to get a second opinion."

Frostbite was uncommon in Georgia, so the doctors were not skilled enough to handle my condition. After a few days in the hospital, they flew in doctors from Chicago, Illinois, who specialized in my situation.

I woke up one day to a male doctor I hadn't seen before by my bed.

"Hello," he said. "Are you awake?"

"Yes, sir," I responded.

"Can you feel my hands on your feet?

"Yes."

"That's good," he said as he walked around the room.

He looked at my mom and said, "The fact that she didn't lose feeling and got to the hospital as quickly as she did is what will probably save her feet. However, we can't make any promises."

My mom nodded her head to indicate she understood. She held back her tears as she came closer to my bed. Her kiss on my forehead warmed my body. I wanted to hold on to that moment where my mother was loving, concerned, and focused on me. It was rare as my mother wasn't affectionate, and her time was usually divided amongst my sisters and I.

The next few days weren't better. I tossed and turned in the hospital bed, not able to sleep most nights. The thought of losing my feet and legs scared me, not to mention, the nurses would come in and give me shots in my backside. I received so many shots I had to lay on my stomach because my backside was so tender.

Even though my mom had pretty much stopped going to church for some time, people came to the hospital, day in and day out, praying for me. More than half the people I didn't know, but I was grateful. Grateful that people cared enough to stop by. Some people prayed as soft as a whisper touching the walls and feeling my feet. Others prayed out loud. They prayed for healing in my legs and feet. They declared God's victory over my life. I even prayed. I also cried every night, begging God to forgive me for anything wrong I had done.

Some days had gone by before I woke up in the hospital full of energy, feeling rejuvenated, and no longer sad. After being in the hospital for almost a month, the doctor came in and said he had good news; I would be going home that day. The doctor said I would be in a wheelchair anywhere from three to twelve months, depending on how soon I healed. He explained I would have to take therapy to learn how to walk again since I had not used my legs in almost a month. After being released, I went home with crutches and a wheelchair.

On my first day back home, I learned to be self-sufficient. During my stay in the hospital, my mom had the landlord make the entryway and bathroom handicap accessible. It was challenging learning how to get around with my wheelchair, but making the house handicap accessible helped. During my first week at home, my mom took time off work to help me adjust. She helped me to get around the house, take baths, and use the restroom. She even taught me how to cook for myself. She showed me how to be independent, even though I was handicapped. My sisters were even super sweet to me. I appreciated and enjoyed the attention.

While in the hospital, I missed about four weeks of school, and my mom was concerned about me falling behind. On the Saturday of my first week back at home, my mother told me I would start school soon. No problem, I thought. The doctor said it would take three to twelve months for me to heal, so I figured my mom was anticipating closer to three months.

It was the following Monday morning when I woke up to my mom yelling from her room, "Queda! Get dressed. You're going to school today."

What? *Did she say I'm going to school today? Hold up. I thought I was going to have more time*—her remarks caught me off guard. I was embarrassed to be seen in a wheelchair and couldn't help but to think what were the kids at school going to say? Was I going to be teased? Putting aside all my thoughts, I began dressing and preparing for my mom to take me to school. I sat at the door, waiting for her to help me into her car.

"Queda! My car can't fit a wheelchair," she quickly reminded me, "The school is sending a wheelchair accessible bus for you."

"The short bus!" I shouted. "No way! Those kids will pick on me. Mommy, please don't make me ride the bus," I pleaded. I begged her not to make me.

After a long time of convincing, I finally agreed to get on the bus. I dreaded every moment. I kept picturing everyone laughing and pointing at me. As the machine loaded my wheelchair up on the bus, I understood what my mom was trying to explain about the wheelchair. I was so caught up in trying to convince her I didn't try to understand what she was saying. As the lift got higher, I felt my self-confidence decline.

I rode the bus in complete silence, praying that none of the kids would see me. As we arrived at

Hutchinson Elementary School, the driver pulled up right in front of the school. The driver and a staff member helped me with the chair and made sure the machine landed me safely on the ground. The driver pushed me into the entrance of the school and explained I needed to use the wheels on the wheel-chair to roll myself to class—I was on my own. I pushed myself slowly down the hallway, trying not to draw attention to myself. I kept my head down, as I didn't want to see the pointing fingers or the staring eyes.

I rolled up to my classroom door and paused before I went in. *Here was the moment of truth.* I braced myself for what was to come, fixed my face, and entered the classroom. My teacher, Mrs. Hartwell, and the students had my desk decorated so pretty that it made me smile. Instead of picking on me, they amazed me with all the love and attention I received! My first day at school in my wheelchair wasn't as bad as I thought. The kids took turns pushing me to lunch, the restroom, and class. I was overjoyed! My teacher explained to the class what had taken place. The kids were very nurturing and concerned about my issue, and most of them thought my wheelchair was cool. Things were good. My mom and sisters were supportive of me at home, and at school, the kids made being in a wheelchair fun. After two weeks, I'd gotten used to my new normal.

My mom returned to work and school, but only part-time so she could help me when I got home from school. She was home every day and met me at the bus;

however, there wasn't enough money coming in to maintain the household. She decided it was time for her to go back to work full time, and that's when things changed quickly. She explained my oldest sister would babysit the other siblings and me. I trembled because I knew this would go left, quick. With past issues between my older sister and I, I didn't feel comfortable.

One day while my sister was babysitting me, she followed me into the bathroom as I pushed my wheelchair. I assumed it was to help me on and off the toilet, but quickly thought about the bars my mom had installed in the bathroom. As I transitioned from the wheelchair to the toilet, I saw a flash! My sister had taken a picture of me. Startled, I was humiliated and felt violated. I immediately jumped in my wheelchair and rolled to my bedroom in fear and wondered what she was going to do with the picture as I had not combed my hair in a while, and I didn't look my best. I closed my door and cried while watching the ceiling. As I laid on my bed, I heard laughter and people talking outside of my window. I got on my knees and looked outside and I saw my sister showing the picture to all the neighborhood kids.

I was helpless and couldn't come to my defense. I cried some more. I called my mom while she was at work, but her boss said she was busy. Shortly after that, my sister busted in my room and asked me for the phone. She took it and didn't give it back. She must have seen me in the window on the phone, and I'm pretty sure she knew I was calling our mom. Hours went by that felt like days as I waited for my mother to get off work. When I heard her approach the front door, I wheeled myself there and cried as I told her what happened. She yelled at my sister; however, that didn't change the fact she still was my babysitter.

That evening, my mom prepared dinner, and we all sat around the table to eat. I asked her if she would stay home the next day since it was the weekend, but she said no that she had to work to catch up on bills. My older sister stared at me across the table the entire time with disgust in her eyes. I knew she was upset that I told my mom about the incident.

The next morning, after my mom left, my sister told me she was about to beat me. I knew she was plotting on how she would get me back. She gave me a choice to drink raw eggs or get a whooping. I was terrified. I stared into the glass of raw eggs and didn't even make it past the first swallow before I vomited. She immediately started beating me in my wheelchair. I had whips and bruises all over my body. I couldn't defend myself. She hit me with so much force I fell out of the wheelchair, crawling around on my knees, trying to escape the brutality. I was hurt, and part of me wanted to die. I begged God to take my life. I asked her over and over again, "Why are you doing this to me?"

Her response was always, "Shut up! You know why!"

I managed to make it to the entryway of the hallway before she stopped, but it was only after she hit me hard enough to make me bleed. I crawled into

19

my room, begging God to let it all end. I closed the door and stayed there for the rest of the day. I hated my sister for being the evil person she was. I hated my mom for putting me in that situation. I hated life period.

Every day when our mom came home, I told her what my sister had done, hoping she would find someone else to watch me. There were times she would whoop her, but that only made things worse. My mom continued to express that she didn't have anyone else to watch me. I could tell she was becoming angry and tired of my complaints. My mom made me feel like it was my fault I was helpless and abused. This further angered me and created a bigger wedge between my family and I. From then on I withheld everything from my mom. I wouldn't talk to her about anything.

Weeks later, my mom came to me and informed me that my grandmother (her mother) had agreed to watch me while she was at work. It took bruises all over my body before she realized how serious things were. If things continued like they were, I wouldn't be able to hide my bruises from my teachers any longer.

On my first day at my grandmother's house, I was a little nervous. Something triggered, and I remembered my grandmother had custody of my aunt's children, the aunt that was on drugs, and her daughter and I didn't really get along. We used to fight a lot; however, I thought anything would be better than being home with that monster I had for a sister.

Despite everything, I gave it a shot, and everything started off good. Everyone was helpful and asked me about my experience with the frostbite. Unfortunately, some old habits don't die. That cousin of mine and I couldn't see eye to eye, and the arguments quickly started.

My grandmother decided she was going to whoop both of us with switches for yelling at each other and didn't care who was right or wrong. I jumped out of my wheelchair and crawled on my knees, trying to escape her and the lashes. When my mom arrived to pick me up that evening, I had a straight face and didn't look at her.

"Mama told me she had to whoop you and that you were bad," my mother said.

"How bad could I be in a wheelchair?" I asked.

"Don't sass me!"

After that, quietness is all I heard the entire ride home. *What kind of family is this? What kind of family would inflict so much pain on a child?* I thought my family had some serious issues. Even after the ordeal with my cousin, I still chose to go over my grandmother's house rather than being at home with my sister; I just couldn't trust her.

Things did get better at my grandmother's house. To stay out of trouble, I would watch *The Price Is Right* and eat oatmeal with her. It wasn't how I planned on spending my time, but it was better than getting whoopings. I remember asking God, "How much longer did I have?"

A few weeks later, God answered, and I had a therapy appointment.

"You depend on the wheelchair too much," the doctor said as he handed me my crutches. "We feel like you should be able to use your crutches."

The doctor coached me on how to stand up from the bed using the crutches. My mom tried to assist, but the doctor shook his head at her. My feet felt so funny, trying to touch the floor. I felt like a newborn baby taking their first steps nervously anticipating falling, yet I did better than expected. It wasn't bad at all. The doctor watched me as I walked down the hallway with my crutches to make sure I was getting the hang of it. That day, I left the wheelchair behind and left the hospital using my crutches. About two months later, I was walking on my own. I had on a bootie, but I was walking.

ASHAMED, ONCE AGAIN

I had an aunt, the same aunt that my grandmother had custody of her kids, that was on drugs bad who we referred to as crazy. She kept everyone laughing and often referred to my sisters and I as the "Onion Family" for some odd reason. One day my aunt popped up over at the house while my mother was at work. My aunt came in and asked if I wanted to take a walk with her. This wasn't unusual since my mom was a single parent, she would ask her to check in on us from time to time. She made me laugh while we walked down Cleveland Avenue, a busy street in Atlanta, Georgia. Even though she wasn't my favorite aunt, this was one of the things I loved about her. It wasn't much of a walk because shortly after we started walking, we arrived at our destination. We ended up at a small brown house with no grass. Even though the house didn't look the greatest, there was a beautiful looking black motorcycle parked outside.

Coming from inside the house, a man about six feet tall, light-skinned, with pretty hair, and a gold tooth walked up and greeted us with a smile.

"Who's the little one you have with you?" the man kindly asked my aunt.

"That's just my niece," she replied.

The man turned around and began walking back to his place. My aunt followed him, and I was right behind her. As we entered his home, I noticed he had two couches in the living room, a rocking chair, and a television. My aunt sat me down in the living room, put on cartoons, and gave me some snacks. They walked into his bedroom and strangely left the door cracked. I'm not sure what led me to turn my head away from the television and toward the bedroom door. Perhaps, it was the noises I was hearing that sounded all too familiar from my experience with Twinkie. My aunt was moaning, and I could hear the man grunting too. I listened to the rhythmic sound of the bed going back and forth against the wall, and I couldn't manage to turn my head back to watch cartoons. I was so engrossed in what was going on I had to watch the entire thing.

After the man finished, I saw him give my aunt money. I remember them having a small dispute regarding the amount, and he told her he would give it to her another day. They came out of the room, and she said it was time to go. We left, and she stopped by the store and bought me tons of snacks before we started walking back to the house. As we arrived back at my home, nothing was said. My aunt waited for my mom to get home, and I went outside and played with my sisters and the neighborhood kids. I replayed what happened, unsure why it stayed on my mind; however, it sparked a curiosity inside of me. Eventually, my mom came home and thanked my aunt for watching us. My aunt left, and my mom cooked her favorite meal for dinner, spaghetti and salad. Afterward, I prepared for bed and school the next day.

A few days later, I was walking from school when a man on the motorcycle passed me and turned around. I worried as I saw him traveling back in my direction, not recognizing who he was initially. I was so nervous the palm of my hands started to sweat.

"Where do I know you from?" he said.

"You're my aunt's friend," I replied.

"Who's your aunt?" I told him her name.

"Yes," he replied. "How is your aunt doing?"

"I hadn't seen her in days," I responded.

"Have you ever ridden on a motorcycle before?"

"No."

"Would you like too?"

"Yes!" I said excitedly.

He drove me around, and then he said he needed to stop by his home. He told me to come in and that it would only take a few minutes. Hindsight is 20/20 because I was so naive. He offered me something to drink and turned on the television. He went in his bedroom and came back out in his underwear.

He slowly walked over to me as I was sitting on the

couch, grabbed my right hand, and put it in his underwear.

"Is this too much for you to handle?" he asked.

"I don't know," I replied.

That was my first time touching a man's penis. I was scared, nervous, and feared that what happened to my aunt would happen to me. Not only did I not know, but I also didn't know what to do next. He laid me down on the sofa, pulled down my pants, and rubbed his penis all over me.

"Are you a virgin?" he asked.

"Yes," I replied.

"Do you want me to keep going, or do you want me to stop?" he asked as he continued to rub on me with his penis.

"Stop!" I said abruptly.

Although I must admit it felt good, I just knew it was wrong, and I was every bit of scared. Every part of me thought I was a grown woman, but now I knew I was still a child. I pulled my clothes up and sat in silence. He got dressed.

"Are you ready?" he asked.

Confused, I responded, "To go?"

"Yes."

"Sure," I said.

He helped me on to the motorcycle and drove me to the bottom of my street where I lived. What was only a five-minute ride, felt like an hour. All I could ask myself was, "Did this just really happen? Am I dreaming?" It felt like a dream. I had butterflies in my stomach as I started to climb down off the motorcycle. As I began to walk, "Please don't tell your aunt, sisters, mom, or no one about this," he said.

"Okay," I said, hesitantly.

I walked home as if nothing ever happened. I remember feeling like that wasn't right. Why were these things happening to me? I didn't want to tell anyone about it. He was a grown man. I felt like I was going to be blamed and questioned about why I went with him? I felt ashamed once again and didn't have anyone to talk to. Because of my behavior over the years, I wasn't close to my family and didn't have close friends I could trust. My mom was a single mother of four girls and often repeated, "I do the best I can for my children." Therefore, I never told her anything. In her defense, this will be the first time she has heard about this. In my defense, she wasn't an easy person to talk to. I didn't feel like I was in a haven.

BEHAVIOR

*I*n fifth grade, my body started going through changes, and people weren't so nice. I was always teased about my hygiene and laughed at about my hair, clothes, shoes, and the heavy acne that took over my face. At school, a typical day for me was going to class, sitting at a desk, and all the kids moving away from me and laughing. I couldn't figure out what was so funny. They would laugh and make faces as they pushed their desk away from me making me the only person in the middle of the class. The teacher would tell them it wasn't nice, and karma would come back around if they continued laughing. But they did anyway, and every day she would say the same thing.

One day, the teacher asked me to stay after school so we could talk. She made sure no one was in the room or nearby before she spoke.

"Ms. Harris, are you familiar with deodorant?"

"No, ma'am," I responded with a puzzled look.

"Well, Ms. Harris, deodorant is used under the arms to help with sweat. During the summer, it can get hot, and one can smell. You might have heard the term —" She paused for a minute as the sound of kids running down the hallway caught her off guard. I could tell this was an uncomfortable conversation for her to have.

"Musty. However, I will call your mom and talk to her about it."

She hugged me and told me to have a good day. As I hurried to the bus, I felt confused as I wasn't sure what deodorant was and why she would call my mother over it. But I had heard the term "musty" before. I walked on the bus, and some kids covered their noses. It hit me. My teacher was trying to explain to me I was musty and needed deodorant. I sat down next to someone that seemed not bothered by the fact I had just learned what musty was.

I sat on the bus, embarrassed. I wondered how many other kids knew about "musty" or deodorant and why no one informed me about this before? When the bus arrived at my stop, I jumped off and ran home as fast as I could as if dogs were chasing me. I knocked on the door as if the dogs were gaining on me and were out for blood.

"I'm coming! I'm coming!" my mom shouted. I could hear her footsteps approaching the door.

"Girl, I thought someone was after you the way you were banging on this door."

I came in and slammed the door behind me. I

wanted to hide my face from being seen by anyone as I was embarrassed and hurt by what happened. Now I knew why the kids made fun of me. *I'm musty!*

"Sit down and let's talk," said my mother, as she broke my train of thought.

"One of your teachers called me today."

"Yes, I know. She told me she would call you," I said with the intention she would hand me some deodorant.

"Oh, you know, and you're acting like everything is okay," she said in a louder voice with her hand on her hip and neck rolling.

Confused to my mother's response, I didn't think me being musty was my fault. I sat there puzzled as my mom said she received several phone calls from my teachers regarding my behavior this week, and I was about to get a whooping. That's when I realized my concerned teacher didn't have time to make the phone call yet.

I snapped out of it when I heard "whooping." I tried to explain why I had been acting out. I was being bullied and picked on by kids at school, but my mom wasn't trying to hear any of what I had to say. I wanted to run, but she grabbed my arm before I could take off. She didn't have the greatest aim with the belt but managed to hit me a few times on my arms. My mom hit me so hard across my back and bottom, I had to sleep on my stomach for the night.

The next day, I wore long sleeves to school to cover the marks from the belt on my arm. Wearing a long sleeve shirt in the summer was just another reason for people to make fun of me. I hated life. I continued to go to school and deal with as much bullying as I could take. I felt like I tried all I could, and no one was helping me, not the teachers, the school, or my mom.

It was time for me to get help of my own. I heard about this gang at school, so I investigated. One day after school, I found them. I told one of them my situation, and she told me they got me. Even though they wore bandanas, I still wasn't sure whether the gang was real. One member asked if I was serious about joining, and I assured her I was if they promised to keep me safe. I soon found out what it took to be a member. They initiated me right there on the spot. Immediately, I felt blows coming from different directions. I cried and screamed, but someone yelled that screaming only made them hit harder. I'm uncertain how many people jumped me or even how long I was being kicked and punched. I just remember laying there afterward thinking *what just happened?*

After the chaos, one girl stayed around and helped me home. My mom had gone down the street to visit a friend, and my sisters didn't pay me any attention as I limped in the house. I could have dropped dead in the living room that day, and they wouldn't have even blinked.

I woke up the next morning sore and bruised from my initiation and left early for the bus stop before anyone could see me. I did not want my sisters to ask me questions, so I wore a hoodie to hide the bruises on my face and body. When I arrived at school, a gang member was there waiting and asked who had been giving me problems. I told her all the names and what they had done. Just my luck, one of my bullies walked past us and motioned to her who it was. My cohort and I followed her and waited until she was near a restroom. There were people in the hallway, but we didn't care. My gang partner yelled, "Let's do it." We pushed her into the bathroom and started beating her. She screamed for help and begged for mercy, but I had none. I tried hitting her as hard as I could, but the pain from my initiation limited me. When we finished, we strolled out of the school, as if we had done nothing wrong. After that moment, I knew this was a legitimate gang.

We ended up at one of the older gang member's homes. Everyone in there had on the same color bandana. I stayed, chilled, and learned more about the crew until it was time for me to go home. I went home as if it was an ordinary day.

The next day, my homeroom teacher told me that the principal wanted to see me. I went to the office, where he questioned me about the bathroom fight. I told him they had bullied me, and no one had listened. He said he would give me in-school suspension instead of out-of-school suspension if I told him who the other girl was. I couldn't give him her name. The gang believed in the "no snitching rule," and the beating for snitching would have been worse than my initiation. He suspended me out-of-school, so I left the building. I knew I would have consequences at home, but I didn't care anymore. I was fed up from taking crap from everyone.

I went home and dreaded knocking on the door, not sure of what to expect. As soon as I knocked, there my mom stood at the door with a belt. I ran down the street before she got a word in. I ran to a friend's house, stayed there for a while, and left before her parents asked any questions. It was late, and since going home wasn't an option, I camped out in the woods. It wasn't long before I saw flashing lights in the surrounding area. My mom had called the cops, and they were searching for me. With me being new to the gang, I didn't remember how to get back to the house I was at earlier, so the cops found me behind my elementary school.

An officer approached me and told me to come out as his flashlight blinded my vision. I was nervous as I wasn't sure if running away would land me in jail. He explained that they had talked to my mother, and she had promised not to whoop me. Instead, she agreed to talk. I came out, and they took me home. I was reluctant because I was sure my mother only said those things just to get me back home. When we pulled up to my place, one of the police officers got out and walked me to the front door. He looked at me as he knocked on the door. I could tell that part of him was in disbelief that someone so young would run away, but the other part of him dismissed it as I was sure I wasn't the first kid to run away from home.

The officer discussed with my mom trying different approaches besides whooping me all the time. He recommended she talk and listen or get me counseling. He didn't think I was a bad child but thought something was going on with me. By this time, I had made my way into my room and listened from afar.

It was the 80s, and my mother didn't believe in therapy. My mother told the officer that he didn't know me. She thanked him for returning me home and escorted him out. I locked myself in my room, afraid my mom would go back on her word and give me a whooping anyway. She told the truth because she didn't bother me for the rest of the night.

While home on suspension, my school sent all my work home, and I was able to keep my grades up. I was a smart student, the top reader, and a math wizard; it was my behavior that had me in a bad place. Had the teachers or school stepped in to defend me, I wouldn't have been in that situation. My teacher that was concerned about my hygiene, finally called my mother two weeks after the fact. Shows how concerned she really was about me.

I was introduced to deodorant just in time at the end of my suspension. I figured I didn't have to worry about being called musty anymore and could focus on my schoolwork. However, when I returned to school, it was hard for me to go back to being the nice girl. I wanted revenge on every person who had ever hurt me. I thought about all the different ways I wanted to get back at people, but with me returning from suspension,

I decided not to start any more fights and lay low for a while. It would only be a few months before school was out, and I would let everyone have it then!

Time passed, and I stayed out of trouble until it was the last day of school. I had my eye on this one bully that had messed with me earlier in the year. I was about to give her a taste of her own medicine until one of my gang members said no. She had her eye on this girl who stole her boyfriend, and she needed help.

"Point her out!" I said. I felt tough and bigger than life. Somebody was going to feel my wrath. She pointed at a familiar face. I couldn't believe the girl who had stolen her boyfriend was sweet and innocent, Tiffany. I kind of admired Tiffany and didn't want to hurt her. However, I couldn't show any softness.

Tiffany stayed not too far from one of the gang members, so they knew where she lived and what time she got home. The plan was to follow her from school to her apartments because we knew there would be a vacant unit next to her place. A member waited inside the vacant unit for us as we followed her home. One member confronted her about the boy, but Tiffany was a sweet girl and didn't want to fight. She wanted no trouble, so she kept walking toward her apartment. As soon as she walked to her door and took out the key, we snatched her and dragged her to the vacant apartment.

Even though the apartment was vacant, the utilities were operational. I got caught up in the moment and took all the aggression I had for my bullies out on Tiffany. After about seven minutes of kicking and punching, we filled the bathtub with water and tried to drown her. She screamed and begged for mercy on her life. The look on her face scared us. We weren't sure if she was dead or not, so we left the abandoned apartment and ran in different directions.

A neighbor must have heard her screamed and called 911. Not too long after we ran off from the apartment, we were all caught on foot and taken straight to juvie. Tiffany wasn't moving when we left, which is why we panicked. The first question I asked when apprehended was, "Is she alive?" They told me they didn't know. I cried as I realized my life was about to be over. All I could picture was Tiffany's body lying in the bloody water.

After hours of being detained, my mom came and got me. Saying my mom was pissed was a nice version of it. After all the yelling and swearing, my mom told me the girl was in the hospital and in stable condition. It was a relief knowing I didn't kill someone.

Before we left, the officer told my mom I was the only one who showed remorse, and it seemed like I was just running with the wrong crowd. That ride home, I sat frozen in the back seat and thought about how I almost killed a girl. I knew I was about to get the beating of a lifetime that would send me to the ER. This had to be my wake-up call. However, it wasn't, and my mom didn't beat me that night. The house was perhaps the most silent I had ever heard it.

Now that school was out for the summer. There

was a lot of time to think. Thank God I didn't get jail time for the incident, just probation. I needed to get out of my environment. The projects were causing me to be someone I wasn't. All I wanted was to go to school and not worry about being bullied every day. I already hated being at home and having to deal with drama at school was too much for me to handle. I wanted an outlet, a safe place; however, all of that was wishful thinking.

Summer ended too soon, but not before my mom had taken me school shopping. I made sure I got the freshest outfits and shoes because I was in middle school, and I had to represent. On the first day of school, I woke up early with butterflies in my stomach. I was so excited I laid out my clothes and shoes the night before. Since I learned about deodorant and hygiene in fifth grade, I thought sixth grade would be different for me. I was into boys now, so my hygiene had to be on point.

Middle school was a fresh start. I attended the same school as my sisters, so that meant we would ride the same bus. I got on the bus and spoke to no one until we arrived at the school. I was excited to get my school schedule and meet all my teachers.

My first encounter with my English teacher was the worst. He was a retired veteran that ran his class-room as if he never left the military. If you were late to his class, he would use an extended ruler and have you hold out your hand. He didn't hit it; he would beat it. During my childhood, they allowed school whoopings from teachers and administrators, and he ran a tight ship in his class.

After a few weeks of school, I realized middle school differed from elementary. I went to a school where gang violence was prevalent, drugs were accessible, and half the sixth graders were pregnant. The teachers wouldn't dare break up a fight. I witnessed girls fighting and cutting people with razor blades. I saw more fights than kids trying to get an education. One day, I heard a rumor that I was to be jumped after school, and I panicked. I thought this fighting stuff was behind me, especially after the Tiffany incident. Not knowing what else to do, I reached out to the gang members I knew from elementary school. From what I'd seen, these girls in my middle school didn't fight fair, and they outnumbered me. I needed all the help I could get.

Word spread because my gang friends came up to the school. They told me to point out the girls that threatened to fight me, and I did with no hesitation. It would be me versus them, and I didn't want it to be me. After those girls saw who I was rolling with, they had a change of heart. They knew they had met their match, and I never had another problem with them again. After I almost caught a murder charge in elementary school, I thought I had put fighting behind me, but I needed help in middle school more than I did in elementary. This school was full of gangs, so I felt like I needed them for support and protection. I would be darned if I went back to being a victim.

The gang came up to school more often after that incident. They picked out innocent victims to jump on, rob, and make fun of. I had to assist, or they would have beat me too. I learned that this was a dog eat dog world, either you are with them, or you are against them, there was no in-between.

I walked around the school as if no one could touch me. No one bothered me, not even boys. I somewhat liked the fact of people being afraid of me for a change. The more I was with the gang, the less I was in school. I skipped school, pretty much every day, until eventually, I only went one day out of the week. I tried to get my life together, but it didn't work. For the gang to protect me, I had to fit in with them, and that meant doing whatever they did. The school threatened to expel me if my behavior didn't change, and if I didn't attend school every day. Since I was on probation from the Tiffany incident, I caught a violation with my probation officer.

When I went to see my probation officer, they told me I had a new one. My new probation officer came out to introduce herself, and wow! She was the most beautiful woman I had ever seen. She walked me back to her office, but during our first meeting, all I did was stare at her. I don't remember anything she said because I was in awe someone like her would be a probation officer. I thought, *why,* couldn't she be a model or something?

After our initial meeting, I saw more of her as she would come by the school to check on me, join me for lunch, and sometimes take me out for ice cream after school. There was something special about her, but I couldn't put my hand on it. I'd never had someone to care about me the way she did. We created a bond. Because I liked her, I asked her a lot of personal questions such as if she had any children or a boyfriend. Come to find out she had no children and wasn't seeing anyone. She answered all my questions and was nothing like the previous probation officer I had. She was nice and kind and always talked in a mothering voice. Not to mention, she was younger, and her hair was always stylish.

One day, after school over lunch, I confided in her about my entire life. I could never express my true feeling with my mother but always wanted to. I desired someone I could talk to, and they would listen—someone who took the time to know me and was concerned with my future. Tears flowed from her face. She told me she wished I was her daughter. I looked at her with tears in my eyes and wished she could have been my mother. She could tell I longed for someone to love me.

After our conversation, she took me home. As we parked in front of my house, she saw my demeanor change.

"Is everything ok?" she asked as she took off her seat belt.

"I don't like it here. I wish I was with you," I said, looking down at my feet, hoping she would pull off. But she didn't. She touched my hand, and I looked at her as a tear fell from her eye. She caught herself and wiped it away.

I told my probation officer I would kill myself if I had to go in there. She talked to me for some time and convinced me to go into the house. She told me to call her on her cell phone if anything happened. The next day, my mom said she was taking me to the doctor. I thought it was a routine doctor's appointment, but to my surprise, we ended up at a mental institution.

"Why am I here?" I asked.

"Baby, I was told you threatened to kill yourself. It's just an evaluation to see what is wrong with you. You have nothing to worry about—if everything checks out."

My mother nudged me into a room where I spoke with a psychiatrist. I continued asking him, "Why am I here?" I didn't belong there. Seeing other kids walking around in straight jackets freaked me out.

After speaking with him for two hours, he said I was free to leave, and there was nothing wrong with me. He suggested my mom get me counseling because it was something internal going on with me. As soon as we got home, there was the icing on the cake. One of my sisters had cut up my clothes. I wanted to kill her, but my mother assured me she would get me more clothes. I called my probation officer and told her everything that happened. She felt bad since she was the one that told my mom I threatened to kill myself. She told me she would adopt me if she could.

I hoped she would adopt me because I wanted to

get as far away from that hell hole as possible. I was tired of the abuse and never feeling loved. Even though I was my mother's biological child, she always made me feel as if I was adopted. Hindsight is 20/20 because my mother was raised never feeling loved by her mother; she in turn, raised her kids the same way. When my mom cooked, she would cover her food and tell us to get away from the stove as if we were contagious. There was rarely any hugs or kisses in my household. Affection did not exist. My sisters and I were not close. All of us were closer to our friends than one another.

The rest of my sixth-grade year, I said nothing to my oldest sister. As far as it concerned me, I didn't have one. It wasn't until quite sometime later that my mom sat me down and said, "Your sister is jealous of you and has been for quite some time. When she cut up all your brand new clothes, I knew something was wrong with her then."

"You took all these years to believe me when I told you I was being abused, and now I'm damaged because you didn't listen!" Her seeing the truth broke me. I cried a mixture of anger and relief. Anger because it took years for her to see how evil my sister was, but it was a relief knowing someone knew I hadn't been making this stuff up.

I called my probation officer to tell her my mom had admitted my sister was jealous of me. I noticed days went by and I hadn't heard from her which wasn't like her. I got a call back from her office, and they said she didn't work there anymore. No way, I was in disbelief. I loved her like a mother. She had been there for me. I looked for her until I found her. I discovered she was let her go because she had gotten too involved in my case. I guess she really did love me like a daughter.

When I got expelled from school for missing too many days, my mom decided it was better to move to another city for a fresh start. We moved to Forest Park, Georgia, for a new beginning. I never heard from my probation officer again.

DADDY ON DRUGS

*I*t was a cold winter day. The type of cold that you dread doing anything besides being at home underneath the blanket. I slept most of the day, and when I wasn't sleeping, I wrote in my journal. Journaling helped me as it was therapeutic to be able to get my thoughts out of my head and on paper. It was hard to talk to my family, so the next best thing for me was to write. When I wrote, no one judged me. I was accepted just the way I was and allowed to express all my feelings without being yelled at or talked down to.

I'm not sure what triggered what I did next. Perhaps it was what I was writing or the fact that when I wrote, I felt free and bold. I put down my pen and walked to my mom's room. As I walked, I was hesitant because she was watching television, and she didn't like to be disturbed while watching television because she considered it her "me time." However, I had a burning desire to know about my daddy, so I prepared for her scowling look as to how I dared to interrupt her.

I was steps away from her room when anxiety accompanied my hesitation. *Would she yell? Would she wonder where this desire came from? Would she be angry at me for asking?* I didn't know what to expect. I could say my desire to know was more significant than my fear. Quietly, I entered her room. Half of me was grateful because she was so fixated on the television that I didn't have to try hard to hide my over-glazed eyes that barely held my tears. The other half was worried about the outcome. I sat on her bed quietly and waited for the perfect moment to ask the question I knew she would dread.

As soon as my window of opportunity came, I took a big swallow and said, "Mom, have you spoken to my daddy?"

"Girl, I haven't seen or heard from your dad in a couple of years," she said, without taking her eyes off the television. Surprisingly she didn't seem bothered.

"Do you know his phone number?" I continued.

"The number I have for him changed, so I don't have a number that works," she said, not breaking focus from the television.

I kindly walked away and proceeded into the dining room. It was just my luck that I saw the phone book lying on the dining room table. There was no hesitation as I rushed to search for my daddy's number in the phone book. I started calling all the last names that were the same as my daddy's. I left voicemails stating, "Hi, my name is Queda, and I'm calling for my daddy, Sonny. I want to know if this is the correct number for him. I have been trying to reach him for some time. I want him to know that I miss him so much and can't wait to see him." I even explained how I was doing better in school and all my accomplishments.

I had to have called at least twelve people. I had not seen or heard from my father in years, and I was extremely worried. After I called everyone, I anxiously waited for the phone to ring. However, no one called back. That night I felt my heart break in half. It was a piercing pain in my chest that caused me to hurt all over. I tried not to sulk in my emotions because this wasn't the first time someone had hurt me. I shook it off, ate dinner, played my video game, showered, and went to bed.

A few days later, as I walked past my mom's room while she was on the phone and I heard her say, "I apologize for my daughter calling looking for her daddy. I had no idea that she had done this."

I felt ashamed, sad, nervous, and happy all at the same time. I didn't know if the news was good or bad. I just knew my mom was on the phone with someone I had left a voicemail with regarding my daddy. I had butterflies in my stomach as I waited for my mom to call my name. Shortly afterward, my mom yelled, "Queda!"

"Coming!" I shouted. I went into my mom's room. She didn't seem excited; instead, she had a "you know what you did" look. I stared her in the eyes and awaited her response, anticipating good news.

She said, "Someone is on the phone and wants to talk to you." I grabbed the phone from her hands quick; I was confident it was my daddy or his ex-wife.

"Hello," I said with much excitement in my voice.

"Hi sweetie," the nice lady said in such a soft voice. "I want to let you know that you have the wrong number. I wish I were your daddy's ex-wife, so I could help you find him. It broke my heart to hear the voice message you left looking for your daddy. I'm praying to God that you find him. Please keep my number and call me when you do," she continued. My heart was crushed.

I heard the sweet lady crying through the phone. Her tears and words touched me that she made me cry. She encouraged me and told me to never give up on looking for him and prayed with me before ending our conversation. I gave the phone back to my mom, broken in spirit as I walked off crying. No other words were exchanged that night. I took a shower allowing disappointment and the water to wash over me. It had been some time since I'd been to church, but I sang church songs and cried out loud, *"Why me God?"* After having my moment and getting all my tears out, I laid in bed. As I replayed the conversation with the nice lady in my head, her prayer touched me deeply. I cried a little bit more until sleep took over.

After that night, I figured I would forget about looking for my father. I did what I knew to do. I was tired of being disappointed. Much to my surprise, a month later, as my mom and I were eating dinner, she tells me she found my dad, and he was coming to visit. She had run into him at her doctor's appointment days before telling me. My mouth dropped to the floor with excitement. I was finally going to see my daddy. *Where has he been all this time? What has he been up to?* I had so many questions to ask him, and I couldn't wait.

A few days later, my dad finally called me. The moment we reconnected, we instantly tried to rebuild our relationship. I was so excited at the opportunity to get to know my father once again. We had agreed he would check in with me no matter what. I explained to him I just wanted to hear his voice and know he was okay. Unfortunately, that promised was short-lived because as quickly as he came into the picture was just as quick as he left. He would go days without calling, even weeks, and months without seeing me. I would call him to no avail, and even at times, the number was out of service. I was hopeful and excited at the idea of having my father in my life. Not to mention, had my father been in my life, I would have never been molested. My anger intensified because I wanted to know *where was he? Why couldn't he keep his promise?*

Months passed, and the school year ended. It was officially summer break. It was back to having beautiful sunny days in which I could stay outside and play for hours. I didn't have to worry about homework, study-ing, or pop quizzes, I could just enjoy the day. It was a Friday, and my mom was in a pretty good mood and decided to take my sisters and me out for ice cream. We were all excited because we loved ice cream. Once we ordered, we decided to enjoy our ice cream outside in the beautiful warm weather. As we were leaving the inside of the store, I saw a sign that read "FREE ice cream for fathers on Father's Day." After reading that sign, it made me angry because I felt the void of not having my father around. The thought of the broken promise came back to mind, and it immediately took away my appetite.

"I don't want anymore. You can have mine," I said to my sisters.

"Queda, you love ice cream. What's wrong..." My mom didn't even finish her sentence. She must have seen the sign and already knew what was wrong with me. My sisters had no clue and kept enjoying themselves and their ice cream. I kept quiet for the rest of the evening. My mom could tell the absence of my father was bothering me, so the next day, she took me to visit my daddy at my grandmother's house.

On the way there, all I could think about was being able to see my daddy. I didn't care why he hadn't kept his promise; I just wanted to be with him. We pulled up to the driveway, and I couldn't wait to get out of the car. I tried to hide my excitement by waiting for my mom to get out of the car first, but I didn't do such a good job. I opened the door before the car even stopped. I walked as quickly as I could to get to the front door so that I could ring the doorbell. My mom was coming onto the porch by the second time I rang the doorbell. I sat there for another minute before I rang the doorbell for the third time, just hoping someone would come to the door for another three minutes before the awkward silence was broke.

"Queda," my mom said in the tone that let me know she had tried and was ready to go. It became apparent no one was home, so we decided to leave. It was such a let-down, and it seemed like I would never get to see my daddy again. As I walked back to the car, all I thought about was the usual, crying myself to sleep, wondering, *why me?* I got into the back seat of the car, and strangely, my mom's car wouldn't start. She tried several times to start the car before she decided to give up.

We ended up stranded in the driveway for hours. I was frustrated at first, but the possibility of seeing my daddy kept me awake. Finally, around midnight, a squeaky car pulled up. It was the type of noise that if I were asleep, it would have awakened me. I watched the car stopped right in front of the house, and my smile instantly went from ear to ear. It was my daddy and some of his friends. As my daddy started to get out of the car, I jumped out of the back seat to greet him but instantly notice something wasn't right. His mouth was shivering like it was below zero outside, but it was summer.

"Hello, baby girl," he said with a low muffled voice.

"Hi, daddy!"

He proceeded to hug me and kiss my forehead. That put me at ease.

"What are you all doing out here so late?" he asked.

"We came earlier to see you, and you weren't home. We were about to leave, but the car wouldn't start," I said.

He walked over to my mother's car and raised the hood to see why the car wouldn't start. I walked right behind him, not letting him out of my sight. He rolled up his sleeves. As he leaned into the car, I noticed a ton of marks on his arm.

"Daddy, what happened to your arm?" I asked.

"I got burned by the iron," he replied without hesitation.

I didn't believe him, but I stood by my dad's side as he worked on my mom's car. He paused for a moment as if he remembered something. He walked over to his friends' car, said something to the guys that were with him, and they pulled off. My dad walked back over to my mom's car and continued to work on it. About ten minutes later, my mom was able to start the car.

"Thank you," said my mom.

"Okay, now you ladies get home safe," said my dad, with a smile, as he looked at me. I kissed him goodnight, not wanting the night to end. I got in the car happy that I was able to see my father but also sad, wondering when I would see him again. My mom pulled out of the driveway and headed home. It was silent until my mom spoke.

"Queda, I don't know how else to say this, but your dad is on drugs. I'm sorry to have to tell you, but that is why he's in and out of your life."

Speechless, I sat in the car, replaying what my mother said over and over again. Even though it hurt me to hear my father was on drugs, I didn't care. I still loved him, and I knew he loved me too! He always called me his little girl, and nothing could change that. I must have zoned out the entire ride because, in a blink of an eye, we were back at home. A home in which I wished my father lived in.

Weeks passed, and I still hadn't heard from him. I tried to get my mom to drive me back over to my grand-mother's house to see my dad, but she wouldn't. Over the passing weeks, I noticed a lot of dads with their daughters. Seeing this angered me and only reminded me more and more of how my father wasn't in my life. I became so consumed with anger that journaling no longer helped. The hurt I felt turned into yelling and arguing with my mom, and I started to act out; I didn't know what else to do with the rage inside me. My mother couldn't tell me what to do. I thought it was her fault I didn't get to see my dad. All she had to do was drive me over there. The rest of the summer was as miserable as me.

My eighth-grade school year began, and I lost interest in school. It seemed like a waste of time. After a while, my mom felt like she couldn't control me, so she would call my dad. Sometimes he would respond, sometimes he wouldn't. I won't forget the day he came up to my middle school and whooped me in front of the class. I remembered that day because he was high, I could see it in his face. I hated him for embarrassing me and never wanted to see him again. That didn't last for long, though, because I yearned for every opportunity to see him. If that meant I had to act out for him to see me, then so be it.

After a while, I started running away from home. One time, I hadn't been home for a couple of days, and my mom called the police, but still, no one could find me. On the third day, I was away from home, my mom had enough and finally called my dad to help look for me. Unbeknownst to anyone, I was hiding out in the projects at my friend's house.

My dad searched high and low and asked people on the streets about me and learned who I hung around. It's amazing what you can find out on the streets. My dad found out about the projects I was hiding in. When he arrived, he went banging on everybody's door, ready for war. He didn't care who answered the door. He would say, "Where is my little girl?" Whatever their response was, he'd push them aside and look for himself. He then let them know that anyone that hid his baby girl would be dealt with accordingly. My daddy might have been on drugs, but he was protective of me and had a military background.

My daddy was going at it for about thirty minutes when finally, word got around that he was looking for me. My friends heard about my dad and told me I had to go. They informed my dad what apartment I was in. As I followed him out of the projects, my heart skipped beats as I didn't know what to expect. I figured he would wait until we got home to let me have it. Surprisingly, after all my dad went through to find me, he didn't whoop me; instead, he had a serious talk with me. He wanted to know why I kept running away, what was causing my behavior, etc. I told him I hated my family and didn't want to live there anymore. I begged him to take me with him. I didn't care where it was.

After our talk, we walked to my house. He told my mom he was taking me to his home for the weekend until things calmed down between her and I. My mother wasn't bothered because even though things didn't work out between her and my father, she did trust and respect him. I thought it would be fun to be with him and grandma. I packed my things as quickly as I could, and we left.

On that car ride home, I was elated to be with my father. I was daddy's little girl. No matter what people said about him, he was still a good dad to me. As my father and I walked through the front door, my grandmother gave me the biggest hug ever. It was so warm and loving, I didn't want her to let go. She asked how I was doing, and we ended up chatting for hours. I missed my grandma. I longed for her comforting talks, her warm hugs, and her genuine love. I was so in awe that I could have stayed up the entire night. I didn't care to sleep. I just wanted that moment to last, but it wasn't long before my dad called me to bed. I obeyed, and kiss grandma goodnight. I went into the room to prepare for bed. My dad slept on the floor, and I slept in his bed. It didn't bother me one bit. I was happy.

I'm not sure what time I woke up, but I remember waking up to the smell of buttermilk biscuits. My stomach was as excited as I was. I crawled out of bed and made my way to the kitchen. As I got closer, I could hear my grandmother expressing she didn't like me sleeping in the same room with my dad. I wasn't sure why because he never did anything inappropriate to me, unlike others. I paused before anyone could see me because the next thing I knew, I heard my dad raise his voice at grandma. At that moment, my mom's words of *"Queda, I don't know how else to say this, but your dad is on drugs,"* came to mind. Drugs can make people act irrational and be untrusting toward loved ones.

I thought to myself, my dad loves me and wouldn't harm me. I enjoyed sleeping in the same room as him. I waited until it was quiet in the kitchen before I entered, acting as if I hadn't heard a word.

"Good morning," I said as I stretched.

"Well, look who's up?" said, grandma.

"We thought you were going to sleep all day?" my dad said jokingly.

"What time is it?" I asked. I didn't even hear what my grandma's response was because I was staring hard at the breakfast spread on the table.

"Chile gone head and fix you a plate, but wash your hands first," said grandma.

I did as she said and enjoyed one of the best breakfasts I had in a while: homemade biscuits, cheese grits, eggs, and sausage. Grandma could throw down, and I ate good. For the rest of the day, it was my dad and I.

We watched television and eventually went for a walk to see some of his friends. We didn't stay long because he could tell I was getting uncomfortable. When we got back to the house, dad, grandma, and I sat around the kitchen table, talking and laughing for the rest of the night.

Those days went by quick, and Sunday came before I knew it. The next day I had to go to school, but I dreaded going back to my mom's house. My dad took me home and had a long talk with my mother and I. He shared his concerns with her that I had shared with him. My mom raised her voice at him and said, "You don't know her. She wants to do what she wants to do. She is not grown!"

She felt my dad was siding with me, but he was merely going over his concerns. The house was cold when my dad left. I didn't say anything to my mother, and she didn't say anything to me. I went to my room and stayed to myself for the rest of the evening. I got up and went to school the next day like any other day. After school, I dreaded turning my key in the deadbolt. I entered the house, sat my book bag down, and proceeded to my room. As I walked past my mom's bedroom door, she asked me to come here.

"Yes," I said nonchalantly.

"Your dad came by here earlier today. He asked me to marry him and to change your last name to his last name."

I was caught off guard, and as I shook my head to

make sure I heard correctly, all I could say was, "Really!"

"Yes," she said with a smile, "He said that we had to do it soon."

I didn't quite understand it all. How my mom didn't want me to see my dad to now her marrying him, and last night she was yelling at him. I didn't care to try to figure it out. I didn't care for my father's last name either, but all that matter was I was going to have my dad at home with me finally. Things were looking up. My mom could tell I was getting excited, and there were many thoughts racing through my head.

"Queda," she said, "I told your father no. I couldn't do it."

And just like that, all those thoughts were gone. My hope was crushed, and dreams were just that again, dreams. A few weeks passed, and nothing changed, my dad was still out of the picture. Since my mom said no to his proposal, I'm sure that gave him a reason not to come around.

One day, when I got off the school bus and walked in the front door. I saw my mom crying.

"What's wrong?" I asked.

As she managed to gather her words and fight her tears, she said, "Your...Your daddy just passed away."

My mouth dropped as well as everything I was holding. I did not know how to react as tears started falling from my face. It was surreal. *How could this be?* Things were rushing through my mind, but the world was standing still.

"What happened to my daddy?" I mustered up the courage to asked.

"Pneumonia."

For some reason, that didn't sit well in my spirit. I felt like it was more to the story. However, I decided to accept what was said. I felt lost and confused. Things were happening way too fast for me to process. A little over a year, I went from no dad to dad to no dad again. *Why do bad things keep happening to me?*

For the rest of the day, my mind filled with random thoughts of my father and my life. *Why me, I asked? Why did my father have to die? Is my life cursed?* I sat on my bed and wept uncontrollably until my eyes puffed. Even though I didn't say a word, my sisters were very understanding and periodically checked in on me. It was rare when we got along, but they showed lots of concern for me that day.

Hours passed before I could control my crying. I sat in the corner of my bed, frozen in time as if I was all alone, and no one could understand what was happening to me. Heck, I couldn't even understand! I heard the door open and the footsteps of someone walking closer to me. My mom walked into my room and said, "I want to be honest with you and tell you what I heard."

"About what?" I asked.

"Your dad and his death," she responded

"Okay."

"I talked to your dad's best friend. He told me your father passed away from AIDS."

"How do you know this to be true? He could be lying," I asked angrily. I was shocked, confused, and battling an array of emotions inside of me. I didn't believe her.

"Your dad got it by sharing needles, Queda. Once your father found out he was HIV positive, he didn't want to live anymore. He wasn't taking his medicine. Part of the reason he wasn't coming around as often is he didn't want you to find out. When he caught pneumonia, his immune system was so weak it couldn't fight back, and he died."

The words "and he died" echoed over in my head. I'm not sure when my mom left the room or when I fell asleep, but I woke up the next morning with the sun shining on my face. I didn't even bother to get up and close the curtain. Why bother? I didn't leave my room, let alone, my bed that day. Paralyzed with the inability to accept the truth, why bother with anything when life takes all that's good away from you?

The next three days were a blur as grief paralyzed me. On the day of my father's funeral, I didn't care to inform my mom of how I wasn't fond of the dress I was wearing. I just stood there, facing the window, mentally exhausted by it all.

"I'm not going to be with you," said my mom as she was putting on the final touches.

"Why?" I responded quickly, as her words snapped me out of my trance.

"You will be riding in the limousine with your

dad's family," she said as she stiffly walked out of the room.

I was very appreciative they allowed me to do so, but I felt nervous and had butterflies. I was sure it was grandma who made riding in the limo possible. I hadn't spent a lot of time with my dad's side of the family, and this would be the first time I would see my half-sister in years; we didn't have a close relationship growing up.

My mom didn't get along with my dad's family, so I understood why she wasn't going to be riding with me. As the limousine pulled up and the door opened, I hopped inside. My sister and aunts welcomed me with open arms. As the car started to pull off, I felt waves going through my stomach. The ride to the funeral was a long one. I didn't know what to expect or how I would react. We pulled up to the building, and they asked all the family members to line up so we could walk in together. We stood there for a while, awaiting everyone. Strangers who I was related to one way or another passed by me to line up. Most were somber, with tears. You could tell who was trying to hold back their tears. Their expressions were minimum and only interrupted by a few sniffles, followed by the wiping of their eyes. As soon as the last family members lined up, the line began to move, and my family got to see my dad.

I was beginning to be afraid to see him deceased. I was fortunate to be able to hold one of my aunt's hand. I didn't remember her too well, but she seemed to have remembered me. As we got closer to the casket, my grip got tighter. I could see the open casket in the distance. My aunt hummed a soft melody that seemed to comfort me. When it was our turn, I got my nerves together and looked at my father. Surprisingly, he looked like he was alive. His head was laid softly against the cushioned pillow, the makeup they had on his face seemed natural, and the suit he had on was nice. He looked like he was resting so much that I wanted to ask if they were sure he was gone.

After the funeral, we went and laid my dad to rest, and I watched them put him in the ground. That's when I broke down. I let out a piercing cry that came from deep within. I cried until I felt like I couldn't breathe. That's when I knew he was gone. It was finally real to me that the father that was in and out of my life I would never see again. The aunt, who held my hand during the procession, stood by my side and allowed me to grieve my father. She began to sing that soft melody, which she had hummed before, and it calmed the raging storm of grief that was inside of me.

Once we left the gravesite, we went to the repass, and I got to mingle with all my dad's family. Despite my not knowing over half the people there, everyone seemed so kind, including my dad's ex-wife. She treated me as if I was her own. It seemed like everyone wanted to know about me except for my half-sister, who didn't seem too interested.

Shortly after my dad's celebration of life was over, my mom came to take me home. I don't believe I said much on the way there. I felt like I didn't want to leave with her and wanted to stay with my dad's side of the family. They gave me the love and attention I had been longing for. People wanted to know about me, I was interesting to them, and for a change, I was the center of attention. However, I faced it and went back to my depressing home.

I grew up with no father figure once my dad passed because my mom never married. Despite what his issues were, my dad was a loving father to two beautiful girls. Unbeknownst to us, my father wanted me to change my last name and to marry my mom because he wanted her to get his military and social security benefits. My father also wanted me to get a large lump sum of money that the military had for him. The only way this could have been done was if my mom was his wife at the time of death, and I had his last name to prove I was his child because he didn't sign my birth certificate. My daddy may not have had it all together, but he loved me.

HIGH SCHOOL

*B*y ninth grade, I stopped going to school altogether. Strangely there was something inside of me that longed for the church, so I started going on my own when I managed to get rides. I hated being at home, so I would stay with members of the church. They were happy to see me in church but wondered about my mom. I opened up about my home life and what had been going on. My pastor said he wanted to talk with me. He expressed that something concerned him after hearing my testimony in front of the congregation and wanted to see if there was any way he could help. He asked me if I had my GED, and I told him I no.

"The first step is getting you back in school," he said.

He offered for me to stay with him and his wife, but eventually, we would have to find somewhere safe for me to live. Staying with my pastor and his family was too close to my home. If I stayed, I felt my mother would find me. Therefore, I would only spend the night occasionally but never stayed an extended period. I knew my mother was looking for me, but I wasn't ready to go back home. Refusing to go back to my mother's house, I ran away again and told no one. I managed to make my way to Cartersville, Georgia, and stayed with a friend's aunt; I was very resourceful at my age.

My pastor called me and told me he found somewhere for me to live, and he wanted to talk in person. After being gone for weeks, I returned home to get more of my things, hoping to avoid seeing anyone. Lo and behold, upon my return, my mom called the cops, and the police arrested me. My mom filed something with the courts that put me in juvie for thirty days as a teen run away.

I had a nervous breakdown in juvie. They locked me up with teen murderers, prostitutes, and people who weren't concerned about my safety or well-being. For God's sake, I had behavior issues but didn't deserve that. That was perhaps the harshest thirty days of my life.

My mother welcomed me back home by somewhat spoiling me, I guess. She surprised me the very next day by taking me to get my learner's permit so I could start driving. We walked into the driver's license building, pulled a number, and took a seat. This man with a baseball cap walked over and took a seat a few rows ahead of my mother and me. I glanced over and shrieked! *OMG, that's my husband. That's one of the lead singers from the R & B Group, Silk.* Anyone that knew me knew I was in love with this man. I know I was only fifteen years old, but something told me I was a grown woman at that very moment. I begged my mom to go over and talk to him. She walked over and said, "Hello, are you one of the members from the group, Silk?"

"Yes, I am," he replied.

My mother came back to me and confirmed it was him. I ran over there, giving him the biggest hug ever. He was the finest thing that walked the earth and more handsome in person. We had an instant connection.

The first question he asked me was, "How old are you?"

"Fifteen," I replied.

"I'm going to give you my number because you are too gorgeous to be fifteen, however, don't call me until you turn eighteen."

I chuckled and cried at the same time.

"Please don't cry," he said. He signed his autography on my driver's license book and kissed my cheek and walked off. He was very charming and kind. I never thought in a million years that anything would develop from it. After leaving the driver's license place, my mom took me for lunch, and we spent a little time together; however, I still didn't fully trust her. Rebuilding trust was a day by day process for me.

I don't know if it was the fact that I meet the love of my life or that my pastor had a talk with my mother, but after that day, I decided to enroll in school and get serious about my future. I told my mom, and we went to enroll in an alternative school.

The excitement of the day awakened me out of my bed. It was my first day back in high school, and this was something new. Not because it was an alternative school but because we got out of school at noon every day. Therefore, I could work, and I did. I landed two jobs. I worked at Taco Bell during the week and Eckerd Drugstore on the weekends. At fifteen, I had money for days.

I was focused on my grades and bettering myself until this fine, well-dressed young man caught my eye. When he walked past me, the smell of his cologne made me shiver. I must have caught his eye as well because not too long after we locked eyes, he asked me out. On top of him looking so good, he was the most popular guy in school, so I said yes.

Being with him was an eye-opener, as he introduced me to luxury. His parents were wealthy, and they were generous to their son. He had a very nice car that complimented me. In the mornings, he would pick me up for school and take me to work afterward. On the days I didn't go to school, I would drop him off and pick him back up. Even though we were close, I wondered why he never took me to his home, and we would always go to mine. One day, I asked why we never went to his place. He told me his father could be abusive when he was high on cocaine. He asked if I still wanted to meet him. I replied, yes!

One Saturday, I took off work just to spend time with him. We went to his home, and when we pulled up, my jaw dropped. This was the first mansion I had seen in real life. The driveway had two entrances with a water fountain in the center. It was beautiful. I got out of the car, and he held my hand as we walked to the door together. I had my man beside me and extravagance all around me, and I wanted that moment to last. As soon as he turned his key to go in, we were in full view of his dad and stepmom snorting cocaine on the couch. They greeted me without even taken a pause in between lines. Even with him telling me his dad did drugs, it still caught me off guard as they were doing it right out in the open.

After they fixed themselves, they hugged me and treated me like a daughter-in-law and gave me a tour of their lovely home. The inside was more amazing than the outside. I imagined myself living in a house like that; luxury looked and felt good. After the tour, we went downstairs to the dining room where they had lunch prepared, and we sat at the table as a family.

The display and spread were nice, but I noticed my boyfriend seemed nervous as his hands were shaking. I asked was everything okay. He replied yes in a muffled voice. Afterward, his dad asked him to take the trash out. I assumed his father meant after lunch because we were still eating. I was wrong. His old man got up and knocked him out with one punch in front of me. I covered my mouth to hide my scream and rushed to his side. I felt so bad for him. I held him in my arms as if I was a momma bear protecting her cub. His dad apologized and said he was sorry he had to do that, but his son knew better. I remained there holding him until he regained his composure.

Afterward, we left. We drove in silence. My boyfriend told me that's why he didn't want me to meet his father. He knew if his father was high and would hit him in front of me. His father's punch swelled the side of his face, tender to the touch. I rubbed his head, hoping to soothe his bruised ego. I told him everything would be all right.

He was being abused, and I felt sorry for him. After that night, I saw him in a different light. Learning that his father was a big-time drug dealer and showering him with gifts to cover up for the abuse disgusted me. I was trying to get away from abuse and didn't want to be a part of that.

A few weeks after that incident, we ended our relationship. I no longer saw him as my knight and shining armor but as a victim. He was a little rich kid who was given everything, and I was working for everything I had. We both had our own struggles, but I didn't want to be a part of his. Knowing how damaging drugs could be, I didn't want to relive it all over again. I learned that lesson from my father.

Our breakup was perfect timing as I got the okay to return to a traditional school and started attending Forest Park High. A fresh start at a new school, improved behavior, and newfound confidence in myself. My body had blossomed into a woman, and I started wearing heels. Yes, I said heels. That was the first time in my life I felt attractive, and the attention I was receiving confirmed it.

My previous relationship was just a taste of what I deserved. A guy named Tim, from the football team, approached me one day after school. White teeth, broad shoulders, nice hair, and eyes that made any girl stare. He was feeling me and trying to see if I was feeling him. He knew I was because he asked me if I wanted to be his girl. Blushing and smiling, I didn't answer him right away because I wanted to see him sweat. Wearing him down, I said yes. In all honesty, I was nervous about dating Tim. Every part of me wanted to maintain my virginity, but he was tempting.

It wasn't long before we were inseparable. He would come to my job on Saturdays and eat and spend time with me while I was working. On Sundays, I would go to church with him and his family, and I actually enjoyed it. His mother would always tell me how pretty I was. His family may not have been rich, but he treated me as if I was royalty. He spoiled me, and I enjoyed every moment.

One day while at school, a girl approached me about Tim and told me she was dating him. Puzzled at her comment, I wondered if she had the right guy. With her smart behind mouth, she assured me she had the right guy. I took a moment to gather myself before I responded because her neck roll made me want to straighten it out for her. I told her he and I had been dating for some time, and I knew nothing about her.

I'm at his house on weekends, and he walks me to class faithfully, so she must have been confused.

She didn't like that because before I even finished my statement, she swung at me. I assured her I wasn't what she wanted. I had changed my life and didn't want a relapse, but she continued trying to fight me even after my warning. I couldn't understand for the life of me why that was happening. The pastor said the enemy would come to test you to see if you have changed. This had to be mine. I didn't want to fight anymore. I was classy, but she made me want to go back to the old me. A teacher came and interrupted us up before anything could go further.

After that misunderstanding, the chick told everyone at the school she would get me. Given my past, I didn't take kindly to threats. To me, threats were promises, so I went home and talked to my boyfriend about the incident. He explained the girl had been obsessed with him for some time, and that wasn't her first time doing something like that. He claimed he never dated her, and I believed him. I would not let that hood rat come between us. Since she threatened me and had a record of acting crazy, I went to school the next day in sneakers and jeans. I felt bad because I knew what was about to happen. I couldn't get over how she approached me the day before.

We had a class together right before lunch, so I knew I would see her. She eyed me from the time I entered the classroom, and where I sat, I could see the side of her face. She kept rolling her eyes at me with a big smirk on her face. Tired of the foolishness, I got up and pretended to sharpen my pencil since the sharpener was closer to her desk. She said something smart, and we had words. Next thing you know, a fight broke out. Something within me took over because I remember dragging and beating her with a hole puncher I grabbed from the teacher's desk. Whatever took over me, was going for death. I hated that I allowed her to get the best of me because that fight caused me to be expelled from high school. It hurt, but I got over it and worked more hours.

With me working full-time hours, I needed a car. Pondering what kind of car would look good on me, I thought about the Poetic Justice movie because I loved that CRX Honda Janet Jackson had. It was just enough room for her, so it should work perfectly for me. My mom and I went car shopping, and yes, I bought the car. My mom actually purchased it for me in her name, and I paid the note and insurance. As long as I was bringing money in, she said nothing about me not being in school. Since I wasn't in school and had broken up with my boyfriend, all I had time to do was go to work and make money.

After being out of school for some time, I fell back into depression. I thought about how all my friends were in school getting their education, and here I was fifteen, expelled from school, and working hard every day. I became angry with my mother for not pushing me to finish. *What kind of parent doesn't want their child to have a good education?*

One day, I walked into my job, clocked in, and then clocked right back out.

"Are you quitting?" the manager asked.

"Yes," I said with no hesitation.

I walked out and never looked back. The very next day, my cousin and I walked to Wendy's to fill out an application. They hired me on the spot but told my cousin they would call her back. My cousin had heard that before, so she knew she didn't get the job. It didn't bother her, though. She continued to be her bold self. She then walked up to the police officer in Wendy's and said, "Can you buy us something to eat?" I was so embarrassed, but he said yes. I laughed at her but was thankful for the free meal. I called the guard "Officer Friendly" because he was such a kind man.

I started work the next day and was excited to be starting something new. I became great friends with a young lady who worked there named Sha. She was friendly and always smiling as if she had no cares in the world. She was so positive even with customers I would have snapped on. One day on a break, we sat down and talked. We talked about where we were from, the stuff we liked, and guys. It was like we had known each other for years, and we were two old friends catching up. The break was almost over when she asked what school I attended. I didn't want people to know I was kicked out of high school, so I avoided the question by coughing and pretending to need something to drink. My coughing caught her off guard because she didn't bother to follow up on her question but was concerned about me being okay. *Close call,* I thought.

For the next three weeks, we would laugh and enjoy each other's company at work. One day, while on break, she invited me to her house after school to meet some of her friends. I said sure, but I was nervous. My experiences with females hadn't been the greatest. We either clicked, or we ended up beefing, but she was a good girl, so I trusted she would have cool friends.

I was right. Sha's friends were all good girls who were smart. They were presidents and officers of clubs in school and talked about their plans of which college they wanted to attend and why. Those were conversations I wished I could be a part of. I smiled and laughed as I listened in.

One girl mentioned how her parents wanted her to go to a particular college, but she felt like she was under so much pressure and wanted to quit. I felt comfortable enough to share my story. I didn't feel like they would judge me because they were so honest with each other. They all went to the kitchen to fix themselves a snack. When Sha and I were alone, I confided in her and told her I had been kicked out of school.

"Omg, go back. What does your mother say?" Sha asked.

"She only cares that I'm working and contributing to the house," I responded.

"Queda, getting an education is important. Let me talk to my parents."

When one girl came back to the room, Sha put her

finger over her mouth to show that this was our secret. It meant a lot she didn't judge me and that my little secret was our secret. The girls came back with some popcorn, and we continued to chat and laugh about our parents. I had a great time, but I had to head home before it got too late.

One week later, I saw Sha at work. She was so excited when she told me she had talked to her parents, and they were okay with me living with them while I attended school. I'm not sure what she could have said to convince her parents, but I thought how nice it would be to do that, but I told her my mom would never go for that.

After work that day, her mom picked her up from work, and she introduced me to her parents. I looked at the father, and it was the manager that hired me at Wendy's. I never knew he was her father. She introduced me to them, and I thanked them for being so kind as to open up their home to me.

However, I never moved in with them. After that, I quit my job. I realized I wasn't a fast- food type of girl. I was tired of smelling like French fries and dealing with rude customers. I wanted more for my life.

Not happy with my environment at home, I didn't want to live with my mother anymore. I was tired of being criticized for talking proper and carrying myself like a lady. My sisters would tease me and say I thought I was better than them and made fun of me over stupid stuff. They always told me I talked like a white girl and that I didn't belong in the family. The more they said it, the more I believed it. I didn't belong with people that didn't love me or want the best for me, so to avoid being harassed and dealing with my sisters altogether, I wouldn't go home. I would sleep in my car and do whatever I needed to do to stay away from that place. I thought about taking Sha up on her offer, but I had already declined. Plus, I quit my job, which was working for her father.

As soon as I turned seventeen, I was out. The police said I was free to leave. I moved in with the minister of music and his wife, which was who the pastor had planned on me moving with before my mother put me in juvie. They had no children, so they took me in with open arms.

It started great even though there were times I felt like we went to church too much. We attended service every week and sometimes two services on Sundays. Wednesday was a Bible study, and Thursday was praise team rehearsal. However, I couldn't complain. I had a roof over my head, food, and clothes at no charge.

The husband was kind. He would tuck me in like a real dad was supposed to; however, after some time, it became a little uncomfortable. He would peek in my room at night and whisper my name to see if I was sleep. I wouldn't say anything even though I could hear him. Not sure why he would do that or what would happen if I answered, but I didn't want to find out. He never touched me or anything, but I always felt it would lead up to that.

After a few weeks went by, he continued to be friendly, too affectionate for me and I didn't get it. I thought he was undercover gay or into young girls. I hadn't met anyone so kind and concerned about me. However, my heart was telling me something else. I felt like he wanted something more, something he should only get from his wife. The way he looked into my eyes, his hugs, and touches told me everything I needed to know. I knew it was just a matter of time. One morning, he gave me bus fare, and I decided never to return. Although nothing ever happened, I later heard things, and it turned out my intuition was right.

SINGING CAREER GONE WRONG

*a*s bad as it was, I ended up going back to my mother's house for a while. This was not the best choice; however, I did what I had to do. Growing up, my mom would preach to us that no boys were not allowed in the house, yet my first day back home, I realized my mom had allowed my sister's boyfriend to move in, and I found out he was paying her a pretty penny to stay there. I saw that for the right amount of money, people would change their minds.

It was something about my sister's boyfriend I didn't like. I couldn't, for the life of me, figure out why, but I didn't get a good vibe from him. Being around him made me feel uneasy like I always had to be on guard. Besides my sister's boyfriend, my mom had moved her boyfriend in as well. I guess people can change when they want.

Whatever they had going on at the house didn't bother me because I was never there. I started working two full-time jobs, and in between work, I pursued a singing career. Singing was always a love of mine, yet I didn't dare share my dreams with anyone, especially my family, because they would only tell me how stupid I was to pursue it.

While working at the grocery store, a man came through my line. I was singing while scanning his items. Singing helped pass the time and break up the monotony of hearing the beep as I scanned the items. I would imagine myself on a big stage, surrounded by fans screaming for more. He interrupted my daydreaming when he told me I had a nice voice. I smiled and thanked him for the compliment. He paid for his groceries and said if I ever wanted to pursue a singing career, to call him. He gave me his card and walked off with a smile. I looked down at the card. I didn't recognize his name, but I recognized the record label.

"Oh my god!" I screamed. I didn't care who was in my line. My emotions were doing the funky chicken. I couldn't wait until I got off work because I was certain I would call him. I told my manager, who I also happened to be dating at the time, about my encounter. He knew exactly who the producer was. I went home that night and practiced my phone call with him. After several failed practice attempts, I picked the phone up and called him. He didn't answer so I left a message. I was determined to make this happen. Over the next few days, I left several messages before I was able to reach him. I had a big grin on my face when he finally answered. I introduced myself and reminded him of who I was. We chatted for a few minutes, and he invited me out to a studio session with a group he was working with.

This is my chance! *What will I wear? How's my hair?* I frantically ran around in circles trying to figure out what needed to be done. I gathered myself, brushed my hair, freshened up, and left. On the ride over there, I played it out in my head. I would sing; he would be amazed and would hand me a contract, and I would be the next big thing! The excitement made the twenty-five-minute drive seemed like it was just five minutes. I was anxious and so full of emotion I couldn't wipe the smile off my face to save my life. I pulled up, parked, and caught my breath. I got out of my car with my legs feeling like jelly. *Get yourself together Queda, and don't blow it!*

As I entered the building, no one was there to greet me, but I could see him in the studio with a group. He waved at me to come in. As I walked to the studio room, I gathered my thoughts and my composure. I fixed my hair one last time to ensure everything was on point. I sat down and listened to the singing. *This is happening! I'm in the studio!* I hid my excitement so I wouldn't appear like an amateur. *I can handle this. This is where I belong.* The group sang their last note, and he called it a wrap. Everyone was full of enthusiasm as it was their last song for their album. I could hear them making plans to go out and celebrate as they were leaving.

"You have five minutes. Get in there and sing

anything acapella," he said, getting straight to business. No hello, no welcome, just go.

I got up and nodded an affirming, "yes." I took a deep breath, gained my composure, and did my best. My voice shivered as if it was below zero in the studio, but I left it all on the line as I didn't want to have any regrets. I sang the last line of the song, stood there, and waited. *Would this play out how I imagined it?*

"You have a nice voice, but you need a lot of work," he said. My heart dropped, but before I could let my thoughts get the best of me, he continued. "You need vocal lessons and I have the perfect person. He's another producer I trust for you to work with. He prepares singers for me. By the time you get back, you should be ready to record a full song." I didn't know if this was a bad or good thing, I just knew it was a start, and I was happy!

I left that day, glowing as if I had made it. I called the producer he referred me to and made time to meet. I was a little nervous that the studio was in his home, but I pushed my concerns aside and made it do what it do. My first time over there, I was reserved, but I held my own. Even though the studio was at his house, it was professionally set up, which eased my nerves. By the end of my studio session, I felt like everything was legit. There was no doubt in my mind that in no time, I would be ready to record professionally.

We came up with a rehearsal schedule, and before I even realized it, I had practiced one song for six months. I thought it was strange because most days, when I went over for a session, he had other girls in the studio and asked me to watch his children. At first, it caught me off guard, but I figured I was just paying my dues. I'm not sure what it was about me, but he trusted me around his kids. He even paid me. I became his nanny, and even house sat. My studio session eventually became nonexistent. My dreams were being pushed to the back burner, so finally, I had a talk with him. I voiced my concerns about why I wasn't in the studio and how I felt as if I was being used. He sat me down.

"Sweetie, you are so great to have around, and I've never seen my children gravitate to anyone the way they do with you. That's why I pay you anytime you help me out. And honestly, I don't think you're good enough for this major record label right now. That's why you were sent to me. I didn't tell you right away because I didn't want to hurt your feelings. You seem like a nice girl with a bright future, but I don't think singing is it for you," he assured me.

"No!" I shouted. "You used me. You used me to babysit while you gave studio sessions to the girls you sleep with. I've watched different girls come in and out of those sessions. Dressed one way going in and another way coming out. I don't believe you. How dare you tell me I am not good enough. You didn't even give me a chance!" I was livid.

I grabbed my stuff and didn't look back. As I left, I kissed the children goodbye because I had really come to love them. As he and the kids stood on the front porch waving sadly, I jumped in my car and sped off with a significant bit of disappointment. *"How dare he tell me I'm not good enough!"* His words hit me. Hearing someone I trust tell me that I'm wasn't good enough made me doubt myself. I felt like I was meant to be a superstar; I just didn't know how to do it on my own. *I now had doubts about my singing career.*

Since I was spending so much time in the studio at the beginning of the six months, I had quit one of my two jobs. Thinking my music career would take off, I only worked part-time at the job I kept. After what he said about me, I returned to work full time. They were very understanding, and thank God, let me back as if nothing happened. After a few weeks of working, my desire to sing kept me up at night. I had to do something. I wasn't going to let someone's opinion stop me. I found a local studio and signed up for vocal lessons to better and strengthen my voice. My first time in the new studio was awesome. A rapper asked me to sing on one of his tracks, and I happily accepted. That was my first recorded song. People were finally going to hear me, and I felt like I was finally heading down the right path.

That one moment had me on cloud nine for days. It boosted my confidence and gave me the push I needed to keep going. One Saturday, my girlfriend called me and asked if I wanted to do a showcase. She said there were big names involved, and this would be a great opportunity to show my talent. I had never sung in front of a large crowd before. However, I told her let's do it. I had about four weeks to prepare.

The mother of an old friend I went to school with was a vocal teacher and singer. Surprisingly, I still had the young lady's number. I called her, explained my situation, and asked if I could speak to her mother. I told her mother about the opportunity and what I'd done thus far, and she quickly told me I needed a manager. She took me under her wings and worked with me diligently to get me ready. The next few weeks were intense. She had me doing vocal exercises and dance routines. She informed me of the things I shouldn't eat or drink as they would impact my voice. I was grateful for all of her help. The night came, and my manager, girlfriend, and I arrived at the talent show, hoping for big things to happen. My girlfriend introduced me to this gentleman that was managing a major production company. The manager was the brother of a young lady who was in an all-girl group from Atlanta, whom the good Lord called home early. He was managing her production company. He introduced himself, and we all sat and talked about the music business.

After weeks of practicing and getting ready, I didn't perform that night out of fear. However, after the showcase was over, my manager left, and my girl-friend and I were invited back to the other manager's home. He told us he was celebrating the accomplishments of his artists, and it would be a great opportunity for him to get to know us more. Upon arriving, we learned he lived with his mother. He explained every-thing before we entered the house. He was strict about us taking off our shoes as his mother had real fur rugs and white carpet. As we entered the home and followed him into the kitchen, we met his other sister and mom. He introduced us, and briefly afterward, his mother excused herself upstairs for the night. We all sat down, and he offered us some drinks.

After lots of laughing and drinking, he told my girl-friend and I to stay the night since we had been drink-ing. He brought us pillows, comforter sets, and all. He was such a gentleman until I woke up at 2:00 a.m. with him trying to put his penis in my mouth. Before I could let out a sound, he put his right hand over my mouth.

"I'm sorry," he shouted. "I'm sorry. Please don't wake my family."

"Well, you should have thought about that first!" I responded as I got his hands from over my mouth. Vigorously shaking my friend, I said, "Let's go Esha, let's go."

"Can we please wait until morning?" she wined, still feeling the impact of her drinking. "NO! This man just tried to rape me!" I yelled, not caring who heard me.

"Oh, no!" she said as if just three seconds ago she wasn't mumbling to get her words out. She jumped up and got dressed. As we were leaving, he continued to apologize, asking me to please not tell anyone because it would ruin his sister's business. I left in tears. I was sick and tired of being used.

Days passed, and what took place that night still bothered me. I called him and asked if we could meet. We decided to meet at the production company where he was managing. We found a room away from everyone else. I knew he wouldn't try me again because the look on his face that night read fear, and he had too much to lose. We sat down, and I got straight to it.

"What would make you do that? What gave you the right to violate me like that? I really thought I had a chance to better my career, but you ruined that for me," I said. "I want the truth," I shouted!

"You want the truth, here it is," he said, "I bring girls home all the time, and they just give it up. I've never had a problem. This is how the music industry works sometimes. You are young and beautiful, so I assumed you were like all the rest. I didn't know you were different. I'm so sorry, and I beg of you to let this go." I could see the vein on the side of his neck, throbbing from his heart racing. I thought about telling him my age, but that would have made things worse. Because of my physical appearance, I easily passed for twenty-one, but I wasn't.

"What all did you do to me?" I asked. I could tell by his demeanor he was ashamed.

He reluctantly said, "I rubbed my penis all over you; however, your clothes were still on."

I vomited at the thought of what this man did and tried to do.

"Do you know I'm still a virgin?" I asked.

"No," he replied. "No, I never would have guessed that. I'm really sorry. I used bad judgment."

I got up and left, not wanting to hear any more excuses. The frustrations of making it in the music industry angered me. *Why do all the men have to be bastards?* That question pondered me for weeks and left me in a funk.

One day, while back at work, I was ringing up a customer when I heard a familiar voice.

"Well, hello, beautiful." It was the producer I had built a friendship with. The one that had me watching his kids.

"Hello. How are the kids?" I asked, slightly missing them.

"They are great! They are back and forth between their mom and me." He paused as if he was mustering up the strength to say his next words. "Hey, I apologize that you felt like I was using you. I was going through a divorce and needed help with the kids. That's why I asked you to take on the responsibility of watching them," he said sincerely.

I nodded as a sign of forgiveness. I could tell that my acceptance of his apology was a relief to him.

"How is the singing career going?" he asked.

"Not well," I said with a face of despair. I looked around, and there wasn't anyone near my checkout line, so I told him what happened the night of the showcase. I asked him to keep it confidential because I didn't want things blowing up. Well, he didn't keep his mouth shut. Later that evening, he called me with another producer on three-way and said, "Tell him what this clown did to you!" After I told my story, they threaten to harm the guy.

That ordeal was draining me, and I wanted it over with. I decided I was through with the music industry and all the crap that came with it. I wasn't willing to sleep my way through the industry to live a dream. If it was meant to be, God would allow it.

HEARTBREAK

or my eighteenth birthday, I decided to be an adult and get my own place. I was fed up with hurt, pain, and rejection; therefore, I went back to my mom's house and started packing my things. I wasn't sure where I was going to live, but I knew I needed change. As I was walking upstairs, my sister approached me and started yelling about something I vaguely remember. I kept on walking because I wasn't in the mood to deal with her mess.

"*Whoosh!*" Out of nowhere, I got a slap to my face. *I couldn't believe it!*

"How dare you put your hands on me?" I yelled.

Her sly remark and facial expression were all that was needed to set me off. We fought, and my sister's boyfriend, whom I always had a strange feeling about, felt the need to jump in. He held me while my sister gave me a few blows to the stomach, but I managed to get loose. He and my sister took off and hopped in his car, but I chased after them.

Part of me wanted to throw a few blows at him; however, I knew I couldn't beat a grown man. Luckily, I found a brick. As they drove off, I threw the brick at his car window. That brick got his attention because before he even got to the end of the street, he stopped and called the police. I wasn't going anywhere because, in my mind, it was self-defense. I guess he thought I was going to be the only one going to jail, but both my sister and I went. I was pissed. I didn't ask for that drama. I was only there to retrieve my belongings and start a new life for myself.

I ended up spending a few days in jail. My car was a stick shift, and no one in my mom's home knew how to drive a stick shift. My mom's car was in the shop, and I couldn't reach my boyfriend—of whom I met while singing in the studio one day—therefore, I ended up walking home. When I finally made it, I packed up the rest of my belongings with no issue like it should've been the first time.

I finally got in contact with my boyfriend and caught him up with what had happened between my sister and I. He made a few phone calls on my behalf and next thing I knew he moved me in with his best friend's girlfriend. She was cool and didn't mind me being there. We both worked all the time, so I never saw her, and she never saw me. It was perfect.

One day at work, I met a customer who wasn't my type but was a really nice guy. However, it was something about him that made me want to befriend him. He would come in quite often, and since I worked the third shift, we had plenty of time to talk. He had a nice personality, and I could talk to him about anything. After work one day, I confided in him on a suspicion I had that my boyfriend was cheating on me. I told him we weren't having sex, and he wasn't pressuring me for it either.

My new friend told me it sounded a bit sketchy, but to be patient and see what God revealed. In the midst of our conversation, he confided in me that he was a virgin as well. I was shocked because it was so rare for a guy in that day and age. I took his advice and continued to be patient. Months later, I got a phone call from a woman, telling me she had been sleeping with my boyfriend, and he had given her a STD.

I wish you could have seen my facial expression. She told me not to sleep with him, and I quickly told her I wouldn't. *Thank God I was abstinent*, but I had so many questions for her. She explained how she had her suspicions about there being another woman and had gone through his phone one day and saw our text messages. She didn't confront him right away but wanted to see how truthful he was going to be with her. She had just found out that he had given her an STD and wanted to warn me before it was too late. She explained that he would be coming over to her house at around 8:00 p.m. that night. She originally planned on telling him about the STD and that she knew he had another girl, but would love for me to be there instead. I was curious as to why she would plan such a thing, so I asked. She said she was tired of men like him having his cake and eating it too. She could tell by the text messages that our relationship was serious and didn't want me to fall in love with the wrong guy. I understood and respected her for that. I agreed to be there.

She gave me her address. This was surreal, I thought, like something you would watch on television, but it was happening to me. I couldn't do it alone, so I called one of my girlfriends to see if she would be down. She was floored and couldn't believe the conversation I had with the woman and agreed to come with me. She wanted to see how everything went down.

I was silent the entire ride over there, playing out every scenario in my mind. *What will he say? Will he admit it or deny it? Was she lying to me?* My thoughts were racing. He either came early or didn't stay too long because as we pulled up, there he was leaving on his motorcycle. He saw me pulling in and immediately turned around. He jumped off the motorcycle, in a panic, and asked me to allow him to explain. My heart was crushed and skipped all kinds of beats, as I thought he really loved me. I knew he cared because he kept holding me and apologizing.

The other woman must have heard him because she came to her front door to enjoy the show. He started yelling at her telling her how trifling she was. She had the biggest smirk on her face. All I could think about was, *"Why did he tell me to take all the time I need before having sex?"* He was only patient because he already had someone to fill that void.

I left that night hurt and angry. He was always very gentle with me and assured me I didn't have to rush things with him. Even when I tried to be intimate with him, he kept asking me if I was sure. I started second-guessing myself and agreed to wait. I thought he had a great level of respect for me. He always reminded me I was different from the women he previously dated. This relationship made me wise enough to understand a man can love you and still cheat.

He would call and text, but I ignored every one of them. I needed time. After constantly contemplating what I wanted to do, I eventually broke up with him. I was still roommates with his best friend's girlfriend. They kept trying to put us back together, but I wasn't having it.

I was back in the dating pool. The friend, I met on the third shift, and I became very close. We hung out and spent so much time together, you would have thought we were a couple. Wherever you saw me, you saw him. It was great to have a male companion to hang out with, and nothing had to be given in return. He was a virgin, which put me at ease because I wasn't intimate either. Therefore, there was no pressure on either end.

However, the more we started to hang out, the more I noticed he started to change. He would bring me food to my job, pick me up for work, open my car door as if we were dating, and buying me things. *"What does he want from me?"* I thought because I know nothing was free. I continued to hang out with him under the assumption that perhaps I was overthinking things, until one day, it was time for him to take me home.

As we pulled up in the parking lot, he started crying and told me, "I love you."

I sat there, dumbfounded.

"Awwww, honey please don't cry. We're only friends," I explained. He expressed his love for me over and over again until I finally got out of the car to end the conversation. He walked me to the door like a gentleman was supposed to. I didn't have the same feelings, and I didn't want to mislead him. I didn't call him for a few days, hoping things would have cooled off and what I said would have sunk in.

When we finally linked back up, he had a gift for me. It was a card with money in it. *"Geesh!"* He's not backing down. Being a young lady, of course, I took it and thanked him. The next week he pawned his car title and gave me five thousand dollars to buy me a new car. There was nothing wrong with my car, except for a few minor things here and there, nothing that would cause me to get a new car. Instead of getting a car, I did what any young woman would do and went shopping. At that point, he knew how I felt about him, but I was loving being spoiled. A part of me felt bad, but then again, *what are friends for?*

One day, when we were both off work, he surprised me by taking me to a dealership to co-sign for me on a car. He wasn't bothered that I used the money to go shopping, but he was adamant about getting me a car. At this time, I had no credit and didn't even know what credit was. He was four years older than me and had perfect credit. He co-signed for me a brand new Eclipse. *You couldn't tell me anything.* I was so happy; I gave him the biggest hug ever!

Days later, my girlfriend called me to say she wanted me to come out to dinner with her and some male friends. She told me I didn't have to worry about paying because they had us.

"Are you sure?" I asked her. "Are you dating any of them?"

"No," she replied, "I'm not interested in any of them, but I know one of them likes me."

This was just what I needed, a night out, dressed up with my girl. I got ready and made sure I looked nice. *Never know how the night may go, right?* My girlfriend introduced me to everyone when we arrived at the restaurant. The guys were very nice looking. My homegirl's guy friend had a nice body with broad shoulders and looked like he played professional football. Compared to her outfit, I was underdressed. If I'm honest with myself, I can't deny that my friend was a bit of a "gold digger" with her evenly toned bright skin and long curly hair. She could have any guy she wanted. I was different and nothing like; I was honest with guys. Don't get me wrong, I had a banging body too, but I wasn't the type to use a guy because I knew what it was like to have your heart broken. I felt bad when the bill came because the guy told my friend I had to pay for myself. She refused and told him, if he liked her, he'd have to take care of my bill too.

"It doesn't work that way, sweetheart, but I'll pay this time because your friend was blinded by whatever you told her," he said.

"I'll pay for my bill. I thought this was something already discussed," I softly replied.

"No, he will take care of it," my friend replied.

I knew from this very night, my friendship with her would become distant. I was slightly embarrassed and bamboozled. The guy was really nice, and he could see that it was a pure set-up. As I proceeded to pay, he said, "I got it next time."

I thought, *next time? Ummmmm.* I continued sipping my drink slowly as he stared at me. Somehow conversation sparked back up, and we ordered more drinks. Several drinks later, we all agreed to go half on a hotel room. Driving home was too far, and we were all not fit to drive. We stayed up, talked a little bit, and then went to sleep. Nothing happened. No one crossed any lines that shouldn't have.

That morning I woke up feeling much better. My girlfriend had already made her way to the bathroom when the guy who paid for her dinner approached me, making sure he didn't wake his friend.

"You seem different from your friend. Let's exchange numbers," he asked.

I was thrown off because this was the same guy who refused to pay for me last night. I smiled and excused myself before I responded, leaving him puzzled. I went to my homegirl and asked her one last time if she was interested in him.

"He's not my type. I just like the fact he has a lot of celebrity friends, and he can get me into all the concerts. I don't have to pay for anything," she replied.

Wow, she really is a user, I thought to myself. I left her in the bathroom, fixing her hair and makeup. I told him yes that we could exchange numbers. He asked if I was seeing anyone, and I said no. I went ahead and exchanged numbers with him. We parted ways that morning, and I left with my homegirl, and I never told her what happened.

He called me the next day, and I asked him about my homegirl. He told me he wouldn't be seeing her anymore, and that night, he realized the type of woman she was. We talked some more and planned to go out the following Saturday. We talked every day after exchanging numbers. He sure knew how to make a girl happy.

I remember our first date like it was yesterday. He prepared me a full meal, which surprised me. He explained he liked a woman that could cook, and he didn't really like fast food. After he made me dinner, we sat, chatted a bit, and let's just say he took me off the single market right then and there. He looked me in my eyes with a stare; you know that stare. I got nervous as he looked as if he was reaching to kiss me, then he whispered, "Let me shower and get dressed. We have plans."

"Oh," I giggled. Partly relieved that he wasn't going in for the kiss. Thank you, God. I was so nervous.

After he stepped out of the shower, he walked into the room with a towel around his waist. He made sure I saw everything else. He had abs for days, and that scared me. I remember thinking to myself, *Lord, please don't let him touch me. I don't think I'm ready for all that man.*

"Thank you, Lord," I said, "You heard a sister's prayer!"

DAMAGED

*Y*arning from the fantastic night before I jumped out of bed and pulled the curtains closed, I looked down at the time and noticed I was running late for work. I rushed into the shower and threw on the quickest outfit I could find. I was working in retail, and opening a store late was a definite no, no. I arrived at work, barely making it on time, but I wasn't going to let that ruin my day. I spent most of my day, daydreaming about those incredible abs and broad shoulders that made me a romantic dinner and took me out for the evening. He was such a gentleman. I wondered what would have happened if he had kissed me.

My staff was continually asking me if I was okay and what I was so happy about. There just a twinkle in my eye and warming of my heart that allowed me to smile. It's incredible how liking someone can change your mood. My guy friend texted me during my lunch break, which made me tingle all over. He wanted to let me know we were going to a party later that night. He asked that I go home, get my clothes, and get dressed at his house. I replied, "Okay." I couldn't do anything else but smile. I hugged my phone as if it was him I was embracing. He made my day. For the rest of the day, I watched the clock counting down the time I would be with him again. As soon as my shift was over, I hurried home.

Leaving home, I gave him a call to let him know that I was en route. He told me he wanted me to meet his brother that night at the party. I was amazed he was already introducing me to the family, but even more so to be out with him again.

As soon as we entered the party, I saw the entire R & B group, *Silk*. My boyfriend waved at a guy from across the room, and he walked over. I assume he was the host of the party as he began to introduce the members of *Silk*, one by one. He introduced one member as the brother of the guy I was dating, another his cousin, the third, his "friend" (which was the lead singer), the other as a family friend who was the second lead singer, and the last one wasn't present at the party. I shook the second lead singer's hand, and we gazed into one another's eyes without flinching. He looked familiar like I knew him from somewhere, but he had on a hat that hid his face slightly. Then it clicked! He had aged but he was the same guy that told me to call him when I turned eighteen. Well, I was a whole woman now and felt the same way I did when I met him at fifteen, but now I was dating his friend and at a loss for words.

Throughout the night, we would make eye contact but would never speak. In the back of my mind, I could only wonder *what if*. I thought how strange it was for me to see him years later, only to be dating his friend. I snapped out of my daydream long enough to enjoy the night.

I continued dating the guy, and our relationship got serious when he asked me to move in with him. Part of me wanted to be on my own, and another part wanted to move in with him. I realized that I still had feelings for one of the lead singers, and I just wasn't sure if anything would ever arise between him and me. It was just wishful thinking, I supposed. I had so many things going on in my brain. After several conversations, we agreed to move in together. I was a little Georgia peach from the south side and knew nothing about the east side.

I was super nervous, knowing that intimacy would happen at some point. One night, he asked me to shower with him. My heart skipped a beat as I thought about the night. I caught a glimpse of his body with the towel around his waist. I could only imagine what it was like without the towel. Lord, help me.

He played some music and turned on the shower. I sat there on the edge of the bed, my body turning ice-cold, wondering what I was supposed to do. He grabbed my hand and stood me up. He looked me in my eyes and smiled as if he was assuring me I would be alright. He kissed me on my lips and made his way to my neck, which sent shockwaves down my spine. I was feeling things I hadn't felt before. It was like a rush of goodness all over my body.

He was gentle with me as he undressed me. First, unbuttoning my blouse. One by one, I could feel the warmth of his kisses caressing my shoulders. Whatever was cold was definitely warm now. He unzipped my skirt and gently slid my panties down. Each inch he slipped them down, every doubtful thought I had was erased with a kiss from him on my body.

We made our way into the shower, and my body shivered as he placed his hands all over me. The way his hands coupled my breasts and how his girth felt against my body, I was inevitably wet, but it was no thanks to the shower. After our exploration of each other's bodies, we made our way back to the bedroom.

He dried me off with a towel and laid me down softly on the bed.

"Are you on birth control?" he whispered.

"Yes, but I've only been on it for two weeks. The doctor said it takes thirty days, so please use protection," I replied.

"I have none," he said, but he promised to be responsible.

We made love that night off *Silk's* music, which was slightly uncomfortable. I was physically with him, but my mind was on his friend. I tried blocking those thoughts out of my head in order to be in the moment. It wasn't that hard, though, because every moment was pure pleasure I never experienced before. The next morning, I was unable to close my legs. I didn't know what was wrong with me, so I went to the ER. The doctor asked if I had sex recently, and if it was my first-time. "Yes," I replied. *Playing with previous boyfriends wasn't serious.*

The doctor chuckled and told me to allow no touching below for a few days. It was a little challenging at first, but I explained what the doctor said to my boyfriend, and he understood. A month later, I felt like something wasn't right as I went to put on my dress. It was tighter than usual and not from the backside. I noticed a pouch at the bottom of my stomach. I sat there staring at myself in the mirror, shaking my head, trying not to imagine the possibility. I heard a voice saying, *you're pregnant*, so I ran to the store and bought a test.

After waiting and waiting, the minutes felt like hours, I looked, and the voice was right— It was positive. I didn't know how to feel. I was happy and sad at the same time. *How can I be pregnant? Why did this have to happen? What type of mom would I be?* I sat in the bathroom until I could make sense of it all. This relationship was moving too fast for me. *How was he going to feel? Does he even want to be a father?* I had seen a recent behavior change and was questioning if I wanted to raise a child with him. I wanted to make sure I made the right decision for the baby and me. I needed time to think, so I waited to break the news to him.

Since our first sexual encounter, he started

becoming controlling. He started telling me what to wear and where I could and couldn't go, and it wasn't getting better. One day, we had an argument, and I tried to leave. I was fed up with his mess, and I needed to clear my mind. Before I could get halfway to the door, he packed chairs and furniture up at the door blocking the exit from me. I cried and begged him to let me go, still not breaking the news that I was pregnant. He yelled and raised his hand like he was seconds away from hitting me. Apparently, he was angered by something, and I was an easy target for him; however, his cousin, whom we were renting the downstairs from, walked in and said, "What's this? Oh no, we will not do this in my house. If she wants to leave, let her leave!" I thanked God for her. She heard my cry and came home just in time. I did not want to be a domestic violence victim.

He removed the things from the door and told her we were just having a disagreement, but she knew better. She asked me if I wanted to leave and I said yes.

"Go ahead," she said, "Nothing will happen to you."

I left and cried the entire time to my mother's house, the only place I knew to go. I was pregnant and had broken up with the child's father. It wasn't too long before he blew up my phone. He called non-stop, apologizing, but I wasn't hearing it. How dare he even think about hitting me? He needed time to think, and so did I.

It was a bit of an adjustment being back at my mom's. After a few weeks of being there, I missed having a place of my own, and I was missing him. I don't know if it was all the hormones or if truly being away from him made me want him more. After being apart from each other and him not calling my phone every day, he was on my mind more and more. When he was calling me, I knew that I was on his mind, but now that the phone calls were less and less, my curiosity got the best of me.

While I laid on the couch, sulking away my day watching daytime talk shows, I received a call from him asking if I could bring him lunch to work. I hadn't seen him in weeks, so I was excited. I got up, got dressed, and got myself together. I haven't seen my man in a while, so I had to be cute, he needed to know what he was missing.

As I pulled up to his job, I saw the gold-digging friend who introduced us with him. I don't know what the hell they were talking about, but the look on her face led me to believe she was still the same old tired gold-digging friend I left, the one he told me he was leaving alone. He saw me hop out of the car, and before I even fixed my mouth to say anything, he immediately said, "She just popped up as usual."

As usual, I thought. Before I addressed him, I addressed her with a neck roll so hard you thought I was about to jump the heifer.

"Do you need anything?" I asked, assuring her that she was dismissed.

"No." She continued to stand there with her thirsty self until he finally told her she could leave. I stood there with my arms folded, and my neck cocked to the side, letting her know that this wasn't what she wanted. She walked on, a little too slow for my comfort, so my eyes stayed on her until she was far enough away. He apologized and told me it wouldn't happen again. I stood there upset but not for long. He hugged me and kissed me on my forehead.

"Babe guess what?" he said.

"What?" I said, trying not to smile.

"I got a record deal!"

"Seriously," I screamed, "Aww, baby, I'm so proud of you!"

"Babe, I know things haven't been the greatest between us, and I'm sorry. I shouldn't have let it go that far. But babe, I want you to come on the road with me. That's how much you mean to me."

I stood there full of excitement with a smile so wide that my cheeks hurt. I was so happy for him and his group. My baby could sang, not sing, but sang. I loved hearing his voice; it was one of the things I loved about him. We made plans to go out that night to celebrate him being on the road and me being by his side. I told him he could pick me up from my mother's around 7:00 p.m. When he arrived, I introduced him to my mother, and they hit it off pretty well. We went out and had a good time. There was no drinking for me since I still hadn't told him the news. After dinner, we went back to his place. He sang me a song and caressed my body until I was weak in my knees. We made love that night and cuddled as we went to sleep. That was what I missed. That was what I wanted: a home, a man that loved me, and someone who did my body right.

Around 2:00 a.m., I woke up to him, punching me in the face. I screamed and cried for help. He placed his hand over mouth and said, "I'm sorry, I'm sorry! I had a bad dream. Shhhhh. Shhhhhh. I'm sorry, baby. I'm sorry." He held me as we laid there. Frighten to death I couldn't go back to sleep after that. *How could I?* I laid there, contemplating our future. I was so uncertain about everything at that point. The next morning, I told him we needed to talk. I told him I was pregnant. Without hesitation, he said, "Let's get an abortion." He didn't want to talk about it or figure it out. Just get an abortion, and he would pay for it. Wow! I walked off and went upstairs.

I had become very close to one of his cousins, so I asked her for advice because she was much older than I, and I was hoping she could give me some insight on what to do. She told me to do what was best for me but see if I could get him to agree as well. She also said he used to beat his previous girlfriend and made her get an abortion, too.

So, this was a pattern. He was a woman beater, and it ran in the family. She explained that most of the men beat their women, and I needed to run as fast as I could. It all made sense now. I knew I had to figure something out quickly. I had to get away to someplace he didn't know. I called my friend who had bought me the car. I hadn't talked to him in a while, but he was pleased to hear my voice. I told him that I needed to get away from some things, so he let me stay at his place while I figured things out. *How was I going to do this? How was I going to raise a child with no father?* Time away from him allowed me to think. It was a few days after I left the house that my boyfriend called and talked me into coming over. I was reluctant but still hopeful. He cooked me dinner. We sat down and talked, but I was on guard, ready for anything to jump off.

"Now that you're keeping the baby, I want us to get our own place," he said during dinner.

"What made you have a change of heart?" I asked in disbelief.

"Well, you could be carrying my son."

Conflicted on what to do. I sat there for a minute in silence. I was tired of going back and forth, and a decision needed to be made. I knew I didn't want to raise the baby on my own, but I didn't want to be in an abusive relationship either. I did what I thought was best for all of us, so I agreed to go apartment shopping. There were stipulations involved, and one was that I had to give the car back to my friend.

I agreed. I didn't stay with my boyfriend that night but went back over to my friend's place. Before I went over there, I called my homegirl to see if she could pick me up from my friend's place in the morning. I asked her to come at 10 a.m., and if I wasn't outside by 10:15 a.m., then she needed to come and knock on the door.

I ran the scenario in my head several times that night. I knew he usually woke up around 9 a.m., so I planned to give him a minute to get up and get dressed. Then I would break the news to him around 9:40 a.m. I stayed on the couch that night, so I wouldn't miss him just in case there was a change in his routine. I didn't feel right just leaving the keys on the counter with a "Dear John" letter. For all he had done for me, I thought he at least deserved an explanation face to face.

"Good morning," I said as he entered the living room.

"Morning. What are you doing sleeping out here?" he asked as he sat on the couch beside me.

"I must have fallen asleep watching television, hence why I am fully dressed," trying to play it cool.

"Okay. Did you sleep good?"

"Yeah, not too bad," I replied as I stretched my neck, trying to observe the clock on the wall. I could see it was 9:50 a.m. It was time to tell him the news; I prayed my girl was on the way.

"I need to return the car to you," I said as I pulled out the keys and placed it in his hands.

"Why?" he asked, filled with curiosity.

I had to break the news to him that I was carrying my boyfriend's child, and we decided to live together. He had a blank stare on his face. He fell in my arms and cried uncontrollably. It scared me. I had never seen a man cry like that. It was worse than before. It was an awkward moment for me and, thank God, my girl had perfect timing. As soon as she knocked on the door, I informed him I had to go. I didn't know what to say to console him, so I left.

It wasn't too long before we found an apartment we both liked. I thought it was the perfect starter home for our family. It had a very nice neighborhood with a playground I could envision our child sliding down the slide. The kitchen was a nice size that would allow me to make his favorite dishes, with a view of the television so I wouldn't miss any of my shows. The bedroom was big enough to fit a king-size bed, and the closets were fit for a queen. I loved it.

Since I had given the car back and my other car was repossessed, we shared his vehicle. I would use the car while he was at work to get things done. About two months after giving the car back, I stopped by my male friend's house to get some of my belongings I had left. I was so busy getting things together for the new apartment that I had forgotten I left some things at his place. We didn't say much to each other, and I was only there less than five minutes. I had to run errands that day and had to make sure they were all done before I had to pick up my boyfriend that night.

I guess he didn't like the way things ended because he went up to my boyfriend's job and told him I was over his house in his car. My boyfriend never called me; he just waited for me to come to pick him up. I finished all the errands and went to his job. Usually, once I arrived, we would switch, and he would drive back home. As I got out of the driver's side of the car and walked to the passenger side, I saw him coming toward the car at a fast pace right over to the passenger side and punched me, knocking me to the ground, pregnant and all shouting, "You better never go to a nigga's house in my car!"

All the employees just stood around; no one offered to help me—no one called 911. Everyone walked off as if it was none of their business. As I crawled to the car, we drove home in silence. When we made it back, something just came over me. I went into the house and started boiling water on the stove. While he was sitting on the couch, I started yelling, asking him what the hell was his problem. He told me how my friend had come up to his job, telling him all sorts of stuff.

I don't know if it was the anger from being betrayed by my friend or how messed up my life was, but I fought back for the first time. I threw every punch towards him I could. I didn't care where it landed as long as it hurt. He dared not to hit me back as I had gone crazy. I was out for blood and didn't give two cents about how he felt. After I let it all out, I headed towards the kitchen. After seeing the water boiling on the stove, he got up and left the house. That night, he slept in the car. I wouldn't have trusted me that night, either.

Unbeknownst to me, my friend was obsessed with me and had been following me ever since I gave the car back. A few days after I gave him back the keys, he went to my boyfriend's job to tell him I was living with him the entire time he and I were separated. He was trying to make our relationship look like something it wasn't to break us up. My boyfriend had kept his cool and never told. I cried myself to sleep that night, wondering what had become of myself and what was in store for me.

My boyfriend came in that morning to shower before he went to work. Once he left, I bleached all his expensive clothes, shoes, and removed all the food from the house. I was physically and mentally abused, and something inside me was telling me he was cheating. No more! I left the apartment and temporarily lived with my aunt, while once again, I tried to figure out my life. I changed all my contact information and abandoned all contact with him. I knew he would look for me; after all, I was carrying his first child.

Everyone told me how he was looking for me and wanted to send me money to make sure I was taken care of, but I wanted nothing from him. Months later, after going in labor and being rushed to the hospital, I allowed my family to call him so he can see his first child born. This was the first time I'd seen tears fall from his face. We realized too much damage had been done to our relationship, and it was best we were good parents for our son.

While I got back on my feet, he agreed to pay rent for my apartment and any miscellaneous bills. He also bought me a new car, so I would have reliable transportation with his son. We still ran into issues here and there, but mostly, we managed to co-parent and become the best of friends. God had answered my prayers. All my feelings for him left, and I was able to be the parent I needed to be.

As he and his group performed all over the world and our son got older, he had us on the front row at every single event. It was challenging for the women he dated in the beginning. They couldn't understand our relationship, but we were doing what we knew to do to be the best parents we could be to our son.

Since I hadn't been with my son's father for years, I pursued my interest in one of the lead singers. I started flying out more to the concerts, and we started staying in one another's hotel rooms, having more visits, and late-night phone conversations. He confided in me about everything; I mean everything. I knew at that point, he trusted me. We both knew we were putting a lot on the line and could have potentially damaged his friendship with my son's father, but *the heart wants what it wants, right*?

I never told my son's father about my encounter with one of the lead singers. It was years ago, so I thought it was irrelevant. Eventually, one of the lead singers and I manifested a relationship, and we didn't hide it. We dated publicly for some time, but I must admit, my feelings were not the same as before. I'm not sure if it was the secrecy of the relationship that made our relationship spark, but eventually, my feelings for him changed. I realized our relationship was strictly sexual, and I was just fulfilling my desire to be with my childhood crush. I did care about him and even loved him, but I realized the love I had for him was more like a brother than a lover.

We both knew things had changed, so we moved on to new relationships with other people. We are still good friends to this day, and his secrets are safe with me.

DECEPTION

J was officially a homeowner! That's right. After living in my apartment for some time, I decided to invest in a beautiful, two-story home in Jonesboro, Georgia. That marked a significant point of responsibility in my life as I was finally able to pay my own bills! That same year, I decided to start my own property management company. I had a vision of what that would be like, and I knew I needed to execute it in excellence despite not having a real estate license. Since the birth of my son, I took to real estate and had managed millions of dollars of someone else's property, so why couldn't I do it for myself?

I became a member of the Chambers of Commerce and met lots of realtors in networking environments. At the time, I did all the marketing and advertising myself in order to maintain my finances. I was hungry and eager to be successful. I really felt my business was about to blow up for me. One night, after work, I was putting my son to bed when my phone rang. It was a realtor I met a couple of months ago. She said a client came into her office and wanted her to manage some real estate properties for him. She told the client she was an expert in sales, not management rentals, but knew someone who'd be perfect for the job. I was smiling on the other end of the phone. This would be my first big break. She gave him my number, and I asked for his information as well. She was clear that she wanted a fee for all referrals, so I agreed to her request before hanging up.

The next day, I received a phone call from the guy the realtor referred me to. We agreed to meet face-to-face and look at some of the properties I would potentially manage for him. We decided on a central place to meet to begin the tour of his properties. Upon my arrival, I could tell it was a good-looking property, and I knew it would be easy to rent. I decided to walk around as I waited for the investor to arrive. Thirty minutes had gone by, and not a single phone call. *Yep, this is too good to be true,* I thought to myself. I looked down at my phone and decided to wait another five minutes before leaving. As I started my car, the investor pulled into the driveway and walked up to my window.

"You weren't leaving me, were you?" He was a tall six-foot, six inches to be exact, brown-skinned male, with lips the softest shade of mahogany brown. I was so struck by his charming looks that I forgot to speak. I also noticed his recent haircut. After staring at him through the window for what seemed like hours, I finally replied, "After waiting thirty minutes, yes, I was!" We both chuckled as I got out of the car and proceeded with the property tour.

As we looked at the property, I couldn't help but wonder how such a young guy like him could own so many properties as he looked as though he was in his late twenties.

"May I ask your age?" I said with curiosity.

"I'm twenty-eight," he replied.

"Well, do you mind sharing how you became so successful at such a young age?"

He shared a little about his experience, and I was hopeful that we'd be working together. That hopefulness turned into reality. We signed a contract, he gave me keys to the property, and we exited the premises. I had my first real client!

"I will be in touch for the other properties," he said.

Days later, I received a text from the investor asking if I was interested in celebrating my new contract with him. I thought it was a very nice gesture, but I couldn't fraternize with clients, I wanted to be strictly professional. He continued asking me over a period of time, and I finally gave in. Let's be honest he was handsome, very tall, and super successful. I was shocked he wasn't already off the market!

We went out, and shortly afterward, we started spending a lot of time together. Next thing you know, we were in a full relationship. It all happened within three months. Just as quickly as I had opened my heart, it was the same amount of time he shattered it into several pieces. *Ladies take notes.*

One day, he called me from a number other than his cell. He left me a voicemail saying to call him on his cellphone and not the home phone. Luckily, I hadn't listened to the voicemail before calling him back, and a woman answered the phone. She asked me who I was, and I told her I was his realtor. She informed me she was his fiancé. I shook my head in disbelief. Perhaps she misspoke but wasn't anything wrong with my hearing.

So, I hung up on his "fiancé" and called him on his cell phone, ready to end things. My anger grew with each ring. *What if he knows I was the realtor and he's avoiding me? Who was this so-called, fiancé, and why didn't I know about her?*

"Hello, Catrise, you there? Babe?" I was so caught up with my thoughts that I didn't realize he had finally picked up.

I took a deep breath, "Yeah, I'm here. So, um, I called the house, and your fiancé picked up? Since when did you have a fiancé?"

He chuckled a little. "Nah baby, we did date a long time ago, but that was way before I met you. She was filling in for me with some contractors that I asked to meet at the house. She was just saying that to throw you off, but there is nothing going on between us."

Something told me not to believe him, but my heart couldn't help but give him the benefit of the doubt. "You know I love you?" he said charmingly.

"Yeah, love you too." I held my face in my hands for a few minutes before going back to work.

Months after, I found out I was expecting my second child, and it was his. I honestly didn't know how to feel. I still couldn't trust him like I used to, but on the business side of things, everything was going really well. I was finally getting into a rhythm with my business and enjoying my home. I was more invested in my career and felt like another baby would just set me back. Besides, we'd only been dating for several months. I felt like I didn't know him enough to be caring his seed. I called my neighbor, whom I was very close too for advice on what I should do. She agreed that it wasn't the best time to bring another baby into the world. Nonetheless, the conversation didn't go the same with him as it did with my neighbor.

"I want you to have the baby, I'd be there for it, I promise." He held my hand firmly, and with confidence in his eyes assured me that an abortion wasn't an option. "There's no reason to get an abortion." He didn't believe in them, and honestly, neither did I.

"I just don't know if I believe you." I had so many doubts, and the last thing I wanted was to be a single parent of two children. Though abortion did cross my mind, something inside of me wouldn't let me go through with it. I remember saying to myself *God makes no mistakes*.

When I went to the doctors for my twelve-week check-up, they couldn't find the baby in the sack. They couldn't find a heartbeat or any movement in my stomach. They told me it was possible that the baby could be stuck in my tubes, and I'd have to have surgery to take it out. I couldn't believe what I was hearing. A bit of hope rose in me. *Maybe there was no baby after all,* I thought. I decided not to tell the father until after the surgery. When the day finally came, I sat in the waiting room, thinking about my neighbor's words. *If they don't find anything, everybody wins. No harm, no foul.* I had to get another ultrasound, which was required before removing the baby. The nurse looked in disbelief, "One moment, let me get the doctor."

"Oh no, what's going on?" I clenched onto the sides of the hospital bed. *What did she see now?*

After lots of whispering, the doctor finally came back in with news. "Wow, your baby is in the sack with a heartbeat! This is a miracle because this baby has been floating somewhere in your body for almost three months."

I immediately burst into tears. I hoped "no baby" would be my ticket out of the relationship. I called my boyfriend afterward and told him the news.

"You know, God doesn't make mistakes," he smiled.

"I'm aware," I responded. My career was officially on hold. I was going to be a mother of two. I decided to go home and rest up. I really wanted to forget about the day.

I continued dating him for the sake of our child, but something still didn't feel right. I had to trust God on this one. This man felt like a mystery. I never saw

119

him go to work; however, he had all this income coming in. I knew a few rental properties didn't create millions of dollars.

I got a renter for another one of his properties. I did the tour, qualified, and approved the tenants. I received a call from them a few days later stating while they were cleaning the refrigerator, they found something on top that they thought I should know about. They refused to share with me over the phone, so I drove over to the rental property the next day. They gave me a bag full of driver's licenses and social security cards. *Oh my,* I thought, *the previous tenants must have been crooks.* I immediately called my boyfriend and informed him of the situation. We apologized to our new tenants and fixed things that night. When I got home, I was greeted by my boyfriend.

"Hey. Can we talk? I've been thinking over a few things," he said.

I sat down nervously because nothing good ever follows those three words. "I want you to know that I'm all in for this baby. I'm not going to be like them other fathers," he said as he stroked his hand through my hair.

"I don't know. I just don't trust you, and what about that 'fiancé' of yours." I couldn't help but eat up every word he said. I didn't want him to see me smiling, so I looked down. He swore he wasn't engaged or involved with anyone and could see how I thought it was something else than just business.

"I know this can be difficult to believe, but just

know, I want nothing but the best for you and my child. Please, I want to be a great father." We continued talking, and I asked where his money came from; he said that he had an inheritance. His answer sufficed, so we talked about the possibility of moving in together. It finally felt like we were getting somewhere.

I put my house on the market soon after our talk. *No more single motherhood for me,* I thought. Boy, was I wrong! After I sold my home, I scheduled a U-Haul to move my things into his house over the weekend. Before the weekend even came, he showed up to my office and said we needed to talk.

"I think we should postpone moving in together," he said.

I could feel my body going numb as he spoke. "It's complicated to say the least," he started fumbling over his words, and then finally, he said, "There's another baby on the way, and it's mine."

I blacked out and started yelling and throwing things at him in my office.

"Catrise, please, calm down!" He grabbed me and twisted my arm back, causing me to break two fingers. My staff escorted him off the premises, and I didn't speak to him for weeks.

He eventually reached out to me, and we scheduled a day for me to go over his house. I told him the relationship was off, and I was only interested in co-parenting. One of my girlfriends at the time was a police officer and also had a strange feeling about him just as I did. We were sitting in the living room watching a movie and talking about how we would raise our child when my girlfriend called me.

"Is he sitting next to you? Just say yes or no," she asked.

"Yes," I said. Now, I was getting worried.

"I want you to pretend you have a family emergency and get the hell up out of there. He is not who he says he is!" My girlfriend had run a criminal background check on him and had the results. What was discovered scared me so bad, I thought I would die in that house that night. I looked over at him, concerned.

"I'm sorry, but I have to go, my mom is in the hospital." He gave me a blank stare as if he knew I was lying. When he went to turn off the movie, all these cameras came up on the television. He had a camera in every corner of the house. *Oh my God*, I thought, *what is this man hiding?*

My girlfriend met me at my house and gave me a copy of his criminal history. He had just been released from prison. Remember, when I couldn't believe how he was so successful in such a short period of time. Well, to make a long story short, all of the IDs and social security cards that were found in the rental property belonged to him, not a previous tenant. He was committing real estate fraud, robberies, and embezzlement.

I couldn't believe it. I shouted to God in rage! "Why me God, why me?" He had money from previous careers and entrepreneurship ventures, so there was no reason for him to have those types of skeletons in this closet. I wanted no part of him in my life or the baby's. I called him and asked him to meet me at the food court of a local mall. As he sat down, immediately, I handed him his criminal background. "Catrise, I was going to tell you..." he said.

"I'm carrying your child!" I yelled. "When did you think it would have been a good time?" Mind you I had just sold my house. I was pregnant and homeless.

When there's a child involved, it's no longer about the man; it's about the child. I had to do what was best for us. I moved into a nice upscale apartment in Atlanta to ensure my kids and I had a roof over our heads. Days later, I went to finalize some things in regard to the baby. When I got to his house, his neighbors told me that something bad happened. They didn't want to get involved, so they got me in contact with his mother. I thought to myself, *now how could it possibly get any worse than the situation we're in now?*

His mother invited me over to her house. I was nervous about meeting her for the first time already a couple of months pregnant with her grandchild. I didn't know his family like he knew mine. I just wanted someone from his family to have a solid connection with. When I met his mom, it was like we had known each other for years. She opened the door with a warm smile, and we talked over a cup of sweet tea.

She told me that he had just been picked up by US Marshals at his sister's funeral for new crimes he committed. They didn't know if he was going to be granted bail because of the serious nature of his offense. I leaned back in my seat, closed my eyes, and took a deep breath. I had made a lot of bad choices when it came to men over the years. That situation was why it's so important for girls to have a father or father figure. A father should be there to set an example for their daughter of what a real man looks and acts like. I didn't have that. That conversation with his mom changed my life. I was able to fully move on and start my life over completely without him.

He called me from prison on March 9, 2005, two weeks before my due date. Our conversation stressed me out so bad I went into labor that very day. I was rushed to the hospital, and Jada Samarra Harris was born at 2:29 a.m., my first baby girl. I worked very hard leading up to the birth so I could take six months off from work to be with her, and it was worth it!

SCARRED RELATIONSHIP

*Y*ears breezed by, and my business kept me super busy with little time to have a social life, not to mention I was a single mother of two. Being a single mom was hard enough without having a demanding career. There were days in which I wasn't even sure how I made it through the day. One day, after working on a major project for a client, all I wanted to do was to go home and relax because I had to get up early in the morning to get right back to work. As I was finishing up in the office, my cell phone rang. It was my homegirl, Shannon.

"Hey, Shannon," I said, happy to hear her voice.

"Trise. Girl. We have to get out tonight."

I could hear my other girlfriends in the background laughing and yelling my name to the beat of the song on the radio.

"I have so much work to do. Shannon, I don't think..."

"We won't take no for an answer," someone yells in the background.

"Yeah, what she said. We won't take no for an answer," Shannon managed to say as she tried to hold back from laughing.

I could tell they were having a good time, and I was long overdue for some girl time. I couldn't think of the last time I went out. I needed to let my hair down, and mama needed some "me" time.

"Okay, calling my neighbor to watch the kids. Just text me the time and address," I said.

"Okay!" they all said in unison.

As I walked to my car, I had a smirk on my face. The idea of getting dressed up and putting on high heels excited me. I was ready to paint the town red. But not too much fun, of course; I still had to work in the morning. I snapped out of my daydream and called my next-door neighbor to make sure it was okay for the kids to spend the night. She kept them during the day for me while I worked.

After the drama with my daughter's father, I found a home suited for my kids in a good school district. When we moved in, our next-door neighbor was always so kind. She would routinely bring snacks over for me and the kids. She would stop by with food and say she felt like giving and wanted to bless us. One day, I invited her over for dinner.

She was fond of my kids and insisted we come over for dinner to her house the next night. We did, and the rest is history. The kids loved her, and she was like a mother to me. Anytime I needed her, she was there!

As I walked the kids next door, I was already planning the outfit I was going to wear and how I was going to style my hair in my head. I hurried inside, laid out my outfit, and showered. I turned on some music as I dressed, and all I could picture was my girls and I dressed to the T, ready to take over. I checked my phone to make sure I had received the address and time from Shannon. I texted I was on the way and checked myself in the mirror one last time before I left. I patted myself on the shoulder and walked out strutting. I hopped in my car and drove to the address she texted, which was a Mexican restaurant in College Park, Georgia. This is not what I had in mind, but I went in anyway. My girlfriends were already there with a table, and it looked as if they had about two rounds of drinks already.

I walked in, observed my surroundings, and took a deep breath as I tried to calm the twitch in my right eye. This was so not my cup of tea. Why did they choose this spot? Women were dressed in their house slippers. Some woman even had blue and purple hair, looking like she was straight out of a comic book. I felt so out of place, and I was overdressed for the occasion.

I politely sat at the table, greeted my girlfriends, and pulled my phone out. I pulled up a spreadsheet I was working on and started reviewing it. I didn't feel like the atmosphere was for me and felt like I had gotten dressed up for nothing. When the waiter came over, I glanced at the menu and ordered something simple because I didn't plan on staying long.

As I waited for the nachos I ordered to come, my girlfriends and I began to talk. They got on me for going straight to my phone and explained that this was our night to have fun. I quickly responded that it didn't seem like this was going to be much fun at all. They all made a face, and we laughed.

I notice three gentlemen at a table to my left. There was one guy that stared right at me. The waiter interrupted our eye to eye contact as he brought our food to the table. I didn't bother looking back over because the moment had passed, and my girlfriends and I were catching up.

I picked up my knife and fork to eat, and right when I took a bite of my food, someone was hovering over me.

"Hello, how are you beautiful ladies doing?"

"Fine," everyone said.

He looked at me, as he stood beside me, six-foot, five inches tall, and bright as the sun itself — his stature caught me off guard.

"What are you drinking, ma'am?" he asked me.

"Water," I said.

He looked at the waiter and said, "Let's get a bottle of wine for this table." All my girls smiled and looked at each other because of his big gesture.

"He buys bottles," I heard one of them say. I could tell he was trying hard to impress us. He was doing a great job if you were to ask my girls. I wasn't feeling it or him.

He began telling me how classy I was, as he observed me eating my nachos with a knife and a fork. I chuckled at him, and as quickly as I did, my girlfriend rolled her eyes at me so hard and mouthed *loosen up*. I sighed and agreed. I started entertaining the conversation in hopes that the night wouldn't be a total waste. The wine came, and the waiter poured each one of us a glass. I took a sip and immediately spat it out in front of him.

"What kind of wine is this? It's horrible," I said.

The guy reminded me that we were not at an upscale restaurant, and that was the only wine they served. I noticed that some of the wine spilled on my shirt, so I excused myself and headed to the ladies' room. As I stood up, he offered to walk me to the restroom. I said, okay.

He walked beside me as if he was guarding me like I was his property, and he wanted others to know. He stood outside the door as I washed myself off. I wasn't in there too long before I became frustrated and decided it was time to go. This place wasn't what I expected, and the wine was horrible—if that was even wine, to begin with—and this guy was trying too hard to get with me. I just wanted to call it a night, go home, and fuss at my girls in the morning.

When I came out of the restroom, I explained to him it was nice meeting him, but I was ready to leave as I had to get up early the next day. He smiled and said he would walk me out. This guy wouldn't leave me alone. I walked off in a hurry to the table and told my girls I had to go. I had put some distance in between me and the guy enough to quickly say to my girlfriends I wished he would leave me alone.

"He's nice. Give it a try," they said.

"I don't know this man, and it's like he won't let me breathe. He offered to walk me to the car. One of y'all need to come with me!"

"I will go with you," my friend Shamrock said as he walked up behind me and asked if I was ready.

I half-heartedly smiled, obliged, and hurried my girlfriend along.

We all walked to the exit, with my girlfriend and I up front, and him behind us. I knew he had to be looking since he was staring me down the whole night. I decided to put my outfit and heels in good use and give him a walk for him to remember me by because that was all he was going to get from me, a view. As we stood outside the restaurant, a car pulled up, playing a new Beyoncé song.

"Oh, that's my jam," I said, as I did a little two-step in my heels.

"Wait right here!" he said.

"Girl, what is he doing?" I asked, as I looked at him, approaching the guy who had pulled in playing my song.

"I think he's buying the CD for you from that man," she said.

Wow, I thought. This man was going all out for me. I mean that wine was a fail, but with Beyoncé, you can't go wrong. That's precisely what he did. He paid the man double for the CD and gave it to me. I thought that was so sweet. He was really trying. Shortly afterward, he and my girlfriend started talking. At that point, I was tuning them out. Then I overheard him asking her if we could meet him tomorrow at a restaurant called "Straits."

Without even being asked, I let it be known that I didn't think it was a good idea. "I have too much going on," I politely said, changing my tone as I thought about bumping Beyoncé on the ride home.

Tuning me out, my girl said, "I know whose restaurant that is. It's owned by this rapper."

"I don't care who owns it. I've never heard of it," I responded.

The guy walked over to me, smiled, and politely asked if I would come out.

"We will be there! Trust that," my girlfriend assured him.

"Can we just get in my car and talk for a while?" he asked.

"I don't know you." The look I gave assured him I was no cheap thrill or a lady of the night.

"I promise I'll take good care of you. It's nothing like that. I just want to get to know you," he assured me.

Not helping the situation at all, Shamrock said, "Let me get his tag number and information. I want you to meet someone. You haven't dated in a while, girl."

Just put all my business out there, I thought.

"I will stay for a little while, but I'm not leaving this parking lot," I told them both.

As my girlfriend left, we walked to his truck. He opened my door and helped me inside. As he walked around to his side of the door, I looked around in his truck. It was clean and smelled fresh. *Thank God he wasn't a smoker.*

I thought perhaps he would be cheesy and try to tell me all sorts of pickup lines, but he was genuine and sincere. He asked questions about me, and if I felt like they were too personal, he didn't get upset if I didn't answer. He kept me intrigued and engaged for hours that I didn't realize the time. It wasn't until my girls came and checked on me, because the restaurant was closing, that I saw the time.

They asked if I was good and I said yes. My girls smiled at me as they walked away. I told him that since the restaurant was closing, it must be time for me to go home. He didn't want me to leave. I couldn't figure out for the life of me what it was he saw in me.

He asked me to follow him to another restaurant that stayed open twenty-four hours. I was hesitant; however, something said he's safe to be with. I followed him, and we sat in the parking lot and talked all night until 6:00 a.m. The more we talked, the more I opened up to him, and we never made it inside the restaurant. It had to be something special about him because I had never just sat and talked for hours with a man. Before I left, he informed me he had to put gas in my car as that was the least he could do. I did not expect that.

He took me to the gas station and filled up my Land Rover, which took premium gas, so it was not cheap! I was still in shock as there was something about him that I liked; however, it wasn't physical. He was an intellectual, and that is what charmed me about him. He sat and listened to me, and not just listened, it was like he could relate to me.

After he filled my gas tank up, he hugged me and reminded me that my girlfriend and I were to meet him at the restaurant that evening. As I drove off, I thought how this six-foot, five-inch guy dressed in shorts and sneakers managed to keep me up all night long. He intellectually stimulated me.

I called my neighbor to let her know I was on my way to get the kids. I would be working from home in the morning and didn't need her to watch them, but I wanted to see if she wouldn't mind keeping them again that night. She laughed at me as she said, "I remembered those days." I smiled. She knew it had been a long time since I had been with anyone, and she was happy for me.

After I got the kids, I waited until I got home to text my girl to make sure she would be at the restaurant. I managed to do some work before I took a much-need nap. I woke up to a text message from my girl confirming she would be there and wanting to know all the details from the night before. After some hours, I finished the project I was working on and took a deep breath. I prepared a light meal for the kids and let them know they would be going over to the neighbor's house to spend the night again. I got them ready and walked them next door and kissed them goodbye as they jetted off to play. I thanked her, and she told me to be safe.

My girlfriend and I arrived at the restaurant at the same time. As we approached the restaurant, a woman walked up to me and said, "Are you, Ms. Harris?"

Taken slightly aback, I said, "Yes."

"Follow me."

As she guided us through the restaurant, you could smell the aroma of something delicious. The décor was charming, ten times better than last night. She told us to watch our step as we went up a staircase. As we reached the top of the stairs, I could see there was a beautifully decorated table with red roses. The plates were set, each with their own menu, and in the center of the table were appetizers with colorful garnishes that assured you it was a pretty penny to dine there.

I noticed a bottle of red wine next to the roses, and from the label, I knew it wasn't the cheap stuff either. My girlfriend and I sat there, impressed. This restaurant was an upgrade from the Mexican spot. We talked as we poured ourselves a glass of wine. The appetizers were on point. Full of flavor, which led me to wonder what the main course would be. A few bites into my appetizer, and a gentleman entered the room.

"Hello, ladies. Thank you for coming. I hope you have enjoyed what I have selected for you," he said, dressed in a nice fitted suit, just the way I liked my men. He was looking really good, and on top of that, he had on my favorite cologne, *Bond*; I knew that smell from anywhere. It took me a few seconds to realize it was the guy from last night. I was in shock. He cleaned up very well. He sat down with my girlfriend and I, and we had a great time. He was able to carry a conversation with both of us without missing a beat. It was through our conversation I learned he was a celebrity chef that cooked for the stars. He was just in the Mexican restaurant last night, hanging out with some old friends and catching up, but he was accustomed to the finer things in life.

He was charming and engaging. He knew how to keep us entertained, and he definitely had my attention. At that moment, I knew there was no need to play hard to get he was going to be mine. Time went by quickly, and before I knew it, it was time for us to go. Like the gentleman he had shown himself to be, he walked us out to our cars. After we ensured my home-girl was in her car, we started off walking to mine. Our moment was abruptly interrupted when my heel broke. I was so embarrassed until he picked me up, placed me on his back, and carried me to my truck. I was loving this man.

After that night, we saw each other every day. It was like high school love but more than that. He made me feel giddy inside, but he loved me like none other. He got to know my children and became a staple in the family. After some time, I told him I wanted him there with the children and me, so he moved in.

He was great with the kids, and he continued to make me smile. However, after a few weeks of living together, I noticed a shift in our relationship. He wouldn't allow me to breathe. I was used to seeing him every day, but he wanted to see me all day, every day. He would come, sit at my office from 8 a.m. to 5 p.m., the entire time while I worked. He would observe my staff and tell me they all had crushes on me. He was convinced that every man liked me. Men just respect me as their boss, I didn't see it any other way.

Once the behavior shifted, I started pulling away, and he drew even closer. He started shopping for the house and cleaning the kid's room. He would have dinner ready when I got home from work and helped the children with their homework. He would make love to me two or three times a day and more if I let him. If you didn't know me and I told you that part only, you would think that I was delusional. *What woman wouldn't want a man cooking, cleaning, and having everything done when she got home?*

Soon afterward, the baby talks started happening. He would tell me that he didn't feel close to his oldest child, so he wanted me to have him a son. I asked him what if it's a girl and he quickly replied that he doesn't make girls. This was a red flag for me. He told me that we needed to go to the doctor to find out why I hadn't become pregnant yet. *What did I get myself into?* I thought. Mind you I already had two children.

He continued to stay on me about it; therefore, I finally made an appointment to see a doctor. The doctor explained there was nothing was wrong with me. It just wasn't God's timing. When she said that, it all began to make sense for me. God was protecting me from something with this man. I was confused as to if he was obsessed or whether he was just in love with me.

After I left the doctor, I told him that everything was okay, but the doctor recommended that we pause from baby-making for a while. I told him that because I needed a break. I needed time to clear my mind and figure out what I wanted to do. I was able to hold out for about six weeks until he said he couldn't hold out any longer.

Oddly, after we started being intimate again, he started talking to me about his past relationships and telling me there was one woman that he would continue to see even though he and I were together. I felt disrespected. *Why in the hell would this man tell me that?* I knew then that the relationship was going downhill, and I needed to exit, but I always stayed silent with him and just went along as if I was a dummy. Trust me; I was far from it.

One day, he came home and announced he was going on tour with one of his clients, which was a rapper from Atlanta, and he wanted me to come. I was super excited to take a break from Georgia. I made arrangements for my kids and packed my bags. When we flew into Denver, we arrived at our hotel with just enough time to drop off our things and go immediately to the concert. Fergie, who was also on the tour, stole the show. She had everyone going in. It felt so good to get out and have some fun.

Directly after the concert, he told me we were going on to the tour bus to catch up with his bestie/client. I noticed as we walked past the dancers, the women were smirking and laughing at me. I felt weird but continued to the tour bus, not overthinking what had just happened. I had a great conversation with the rapper and everyone on the tour bus. We were talking about the show, cracking jokes, and all the behind the scene stuff. After some time, his ex was brought up in the conversation. They had a full-blown discussion as if I wasn't sitting there. This man didn't bother to stop or change the conversation at all. I sat in silence and said nothing. I was hurt.

Then there was a knock on the door that made them stop talking. It was his cousin. I was so excited to see him, as he was a familiar and comforting face in this uncomfortable situation. I was excited until my man instructed him to take me back to the hotel. I wanted to go with him to the after party, but I didn't get out of character or make a scene. I had come too far from that. This man left me with his relatives in a hotel all night and never came back until 6 a.m. the next morning. I knew when I got back to Atlanta, it was over. He knew it too. I left and never looked back.

I was amazed by how much I found out about him after we lived together. Little did I know, he had three addresses. He still had a lease in his name with his ex-girlfriend, which I also found out was the rapper's first cousin. I should have known it was too good to be true. I had to move on and put that mess behind me. About a month later, I started dating someone else. We had known each other for years, and he was fond of me. We would go out from time to time but nothing too serious. I was still trying to heal, and it was a process. Every time I thought of my ex, I would try to block him out of my mind, but I couldn't deny my love for him.

I knew it was toxic, and I should have run while I had the chance. Even though I was dating someone, I still considered myself single and let my ex back into my life. We picked right back up where we left off, and sadly, things got worse. Little did I know, he purposely came back to hurt me. I was the first woman that left him, and that did not sit well with him.

He had people following me everywhere I went. I had no privacy. I started feeling like I never would escape this man or his reach. My friends were concerned about my well-being because they had never seen me act that way. I needed to get away, so I did the best thing I could think of. I packed up and moved forty minutes away to an entirely different side of town where no one knew me, and I figured I would be safe from him. Foolish, I know.

I stayed hidden for months, and I felt like things were getting better when all of a sudden, I received a text message. I had erased his name out of my phone, so I wasn't quite sure who he was, but the history of our conversations was there. The memories came back of how he made me feel when we were together—the good times. I put my phone down and walked away, but the more I paced, the urge to reply became stronger. I missed him. I missed us. Not too long after I replied back, he was back into my life.

We took it slow, and I eventually allowed him to stay the night with me. He would take the kids to school, cook breakfast, and it just felt good to know we were back in a good place. He even helped decorate my new condo. It was going good until one day I found out he had a baby. That devastated me. I pictured us being a family. I knew then that I had to take precautions. I wanted us to be together, but I didn't want to have any more children. I decided to draw up a contract while he was out of town on business indicating he would agree to pay for an abortion and provide counseling services if I got pregnant.

He was scheduled to be back in town in a few days, and I figured I would ask him to sign it then. I would make sure the kids were away. I just needed the perfect time. I debated if I should play it cool, act like I didn't know he had another child, and see if he would tell me, or should I go "Waiting to Exhale" on him. All the while he was out of town, we talked and texted, but I never mentioned anything about his child. I wanted to, but I had to figure out my angle.

He called me to let me know he landed safe and was on his way to my house. Here was my chance.

Before he even got a chance to sit down, I didn't waste any time.

"You have a baby? How could you do this to me?" I yelled.

"It's not what you think. She was getting older and wanted to have a baby. We've been knowing one another since we were young. She is a good friend, so I agreed," he replied.

"Stop with your lies and just tell the truth!" I cried out. I was so hurt that it felt like my heart broke. I fell down and just sobbed.

"Babe, I told you I wanted a son. Just know that you're the only woman I've ever wanted to marry, and we will," he said, soothing every broken part of me.

Knowing that he had a child by someone else was painful, yet I still loved him and wanted to be his wife. We laid in bed that night, and I told him I had something I wanted him to sign. I had an abortion agreement. It went against my beliefs, but I had to be rational. The abortion agreement stated if I ever became pregnant with his child, I didn't want it. He would provide therapy for my emotional support, and he would pay full cost for the abortion. Since we had been together for years, we didn't use protection. Birth control could take a while to be effective, and I knew I didn't want any children with him after I saw how he neglected his other children.

He refused to sign it, so I had my own plan of action. I was going to take Plan B pills.

The very next morning, I had a flight to catch, and he offered to fix me breakfast before I left. He made omelets, which I loved. I thanked him and gave him a hug and kiss goodbye. I left a little earlier so I can stop by the drug to get my Plan B pill from the pharmacy. About halfway to the airport, my stomach started to hurt and growl. I still tried making it; however, as I pulled into the airport, I had a bowel movement all over myself. I was embarrassed and clearly could not board a plane in that condition. I missed my flight and came back home only to find he had already left. Thank God, I wouldn't want him to have seen me like that.

I quickly showered, changed, and called my doctor. I figured maybe the Plan B didn't agree with me, but I'd rather be safe than sorry. As gross as it was, I had to take a sample of my stool with me to the doctor. My doctor informed me that it could take up to a week to get back the results. I made some arrangements and ended up catching a flight later that evening. I was not going to miss my R & B Silk family performance.

After enjoying the concert and arriving back in Atlanta, I came back home to a spotless house. Everything was immaculate. He told me he wanted to surprise me, so he cleaned. After putting my bags down, he said he wanted to talk to me. He told me while I was gone, someone came to my house and loosened up the bolts on his tires, and he didn't want to have to shoot anyone. I was not dating anyone else at that time, so I knew that couldn't be true. I explained I had cameras around the property, and I would take a look.

"No, you don't have to do that!" he quickly shouted. "I just wanted you to know."

I left it alone for the rest of the evening, but things didn't sit well with me, so I decided to look at the cameras. I discovered no one had ever come to my home or near it. After this incident, I started catching him in so many lies I knew it was time for me to get him out of my life, permanently.

I received the report a week later and was informed that laxatives were discovered in my stool. I had never taken laxatives. Laxatives must have been placed in my food on purpose and would explain why I got sick. That report sealed the deal. Not sure what kind of hold this man had on me, but I was serious and desperate for a change.

It took me a while to figure out why I couldn't get this man out of my system. Well, deep down inside, I knew why. I was just too embarrassed to tell anyone about it. He was a "Blood Hound." If you don't know what it is, Google it. It's very dangerous, ladies. I encourage you to be very careful when you're lying down with your mates. If something seems abnormal in the bedroom, that means it is.

I became intimate with this man one last time after my birthday, and I was one hundred percent sure that would be our last time. I had just started dating someone I had been friends with for years, and I wanted to give it a chance. I was tired of being cheated on with multiple women and accepting the abuse. Three weeks later, I missed my period. I knew I was pregnant. I took three tests, and they were all positive. I guess my Plan B didn't work. He seemed excited when I called and told him and even went to the doctor with me.

A week later, I started to get threats about what would happen if I didn't go through with an abortion. *What in the world just happened?* I was sure that this man was bi-polar. I didn't care about his threats. Honestly, I was doing so well for myself. I didn't want any more children. I tried to abort, but the good Lord wouldn't let me. The guilt was too much to bear. I didn't feel like I could live with myself knowing I was murdering a child. I decided to keep my baby. After I made the decision, he threatened me more.

I was serious about keeping my child, so I found a lawyer that could help me file for child support and get a paternity test. If he didn't want to be physically in his child's life, at least he could be financially. After my lawyer informed me that the paperwork had been filed, I noticed a decline in his calls. I was nervous that he wouldn't show up in court the day of the hearing, but to my surprise, he appeared. I explained my case, and he explained his. He even had the nerve to say he told me to get an abortion. The judge made his decision and placed him on child support. He told the judge outright he wasn't paying it. He had some nerve, but that was okay. His outbursts got him arrested right there in the courtroom.

I found out later that he had married and relocated out of state. He never tried to meet his one and only baby girl. All the signs were there. I just missed them because I was blindly in love. God spared me from getting pregnant, and I continued to go against him. I ignored all the warning signs because I was led astray by my lustful desires. Therefore, I went through my entire pregnancy alone with no support from him.

DEPRESSION, HEALTH SCARE

The coldness of my room sent chills down my spine as I stepped foot on my hardwood floors. I slid on my slippers that warmed my aching feet as I made it to the restroom. My decision to go through with the pregnancy finally had kicked in. I would go from happy to sad; my emotions were all over the place. I asked myself daily *did I make the right decision?* I was already raising two children as a single mother. *Lord, what did I get myself into?* However, I couldn't see myself taking the life of an innocent child.

As time went on, I got sick to the point that I couldn't even work. I started living off my savings. It wasn't long before that started to run low. After a while, I started having financial problems. I exhausted every loan possible and borrowed all the money I could. I was robbing Peter to pay Paul. With all the worrying and stressing, depression started to take a toll on me. I couldn't see the light at the end of this tunnel.

Five months into my pregnancy, the sickness wore off. My body made sure to make up for every day that I could not eat. I started to crave things I had never eaten in my life; instead of eating a few slices of pizza, I would eat an entire box. I couldn't just have one soda; I would drink the whole six-pack. I had pregnancy cravings before, but this was not the norm for me. It was so extreme I gained almost fifty pounds in one month. In my depressed state, I didn't care to leave the house, and I didn't feel like being bothered by anyone. I would just wallow in my sorrow. If it weren't for me having check-ups with the doctor, I wouldn't have left my home at all.

When I arrived at my doctor's office, I could tell from the look on his face that he was in utter shock once he realized who I was. My doctor had a long conversation with me and explained this would not turn out good if I didn't control my weight. His words hit me, and tears started flowing from my face. Trying to gather my words, I assured him that I was making an effort, but I was hungry all the time, and with all that I was going through, food was my only comfort. He placed me on a diet, salad and fruit only, nothing else, with lots of water. He assured me that following his instructions was critical for not only my health but for the health of the baby as well.

I sat there, sobbing because it was never my intention to let my weight get out of control, but the cravings wouldn't go away. I didn't realize that it had gotten that bad. To monitor my health and to make sure I adhered to his instructions, the doctor scheduled weekly visits, instead of monthly, and appointed me a nutritionist and a specialist. Even with having a team to help me lose weight, my weight didn't get better. Nothing they tried worked. Every week I went back, I had gained ten pounds.

By the time I was eight months, I had gained one hundred and fifty pounds. I weighed two hundred and eighty pounds, which was more than double my normal weight. The doctors could not understand why I was putting on so much weight. The nurses told me I would have high blood pressure, diabetes, and a list of other problems if I did not change my habits quickly. My baby, at that point, was already eight pounds, and by the time I was nine months, it would weigh ten pounds. With my average weight only being one hundred and thirty pounds, my doctor felt I would die and go into cardiac arrest, trying to push a baby that size out. He recommended a C- Section; however, I refused. I birthed my other children naturally, and I wanted the same for my third child. I didn't have any health problems, so I felt I could do it.

Well, little did I know, my doctor was right! I didn't have any health problems during the pregnancy or while giving birth; however, it was afterward that my health issues began. I didn't feel like the baby was out of me. I told the nurse how I was feeling, but I was eventually released. A few days later, I was home in the bed with my newborn and carrying for my other children and my niece when it felt like an elephant was on my chest. It took everything in me to call out for my son and tell him to call 911. When he entered my room, he could tell something was wrong with me, and by the look on his face, he was scared. Seeing him look that way, scared me. My body was weak, my chest was tight, and I felt light-headed. It started to become hard for me to swallow.

The first on the scene was the fire truck. I could hear the loud sirens as they entered the neighborhood. My son ran to the front door and guided them to my room. The fireman ran into my room and began asking me about my symptoms and flashed a light into my eyes.

"Tell me I'm not dying. If not, I'm staying right here with my children," I gasped, almost choking on my words.

"I wish we could tell you that, however, you're on the verge of a stroke right now," the fireman said as he signaled for the EMT arriving to bring in the gurney.

"We need to get you to the hospital. Your blood pressure is double the normal range. Whom can you call to come to stay with your children?" he continued.

"My ma... mother," I signaled to my son to bring me the phone. I called my mother, barely able to press the buttons.

"Mom, I need you to watch the kids. I'm heading to the hospital. The medic said I could have a stroke at any time," I said.

"I don't have any clothes on. I have to get dressed," my mother responded.

"Mom, I could be dying," I pleaded with her.

"I heard you," she sharply replied.

The pain intensified, and I cried. Reality began to kick in. This could be the last time I see my kids. This could be the last time I hold my daughter. This was all surreal. I wanted my life to be normal. I didn't want to be depressed or overweight. I wanted my kids and I to be happy. I wanted to enjoy life. At that very moment, life was fleeting.

"We have to get her to a hospital. Her crying is going to send her into cardiac arrest. Her pressure is going higher," said the medic.

"Ms. Harris, the fire department will have to stay in your home with your children until your mother arrives. I want to be honest with you. You will die here if we don't get you to the hospital. Your heart is not pumping normally," someone said.

"My newborn baby. No, I'm breastfeeding. I can't leave her," I yelled. I didn't want to go. I wanted to stay. My kids were the only thing on my mind.

"Ma'am. You won't be here to breastfeed. We have to go now. Please stop crying; your pressure is going higher and higher. You will not make it to the hospital," someone said as the EMTs lifted me on the stretcher.

Upon arriving at the hospital, they placed me in a room. They worked on me for some time, but my blood pressure would not stabilize; therefore, they rushed me to ICU. I was scared out of my mind. I didn't know what was going to happen to me. All I could do was pray and hope for the best. That wasn't how I wanted things to end for me.

The hospital called my emergency contacts to notify them of my situation. The nurse informed me when my family arrived and wanted to make sure I was okay with having guests. My sister and aunts on my dad's side of my family were there, alongside some close friends. Seeing them did me some good. They spoke words of encouragement and prayed for me. They asked about the kids and to see if there was anything they could do. No one from my mom's side came except for my niece.

I was in ICU for a few days before they transferred me to a regular room. I was glad to see that things were getting better. My family and friends continued to check on me. My sister informed me that she had my kids and had been watching them since my mother called her and told her what happened on the day of the incident. Sadly, at that point, my mother had yet to visit me in the hospital. I had company in my room when the hospital phone rang.

"Hello?" I said, wondering who would be calling me.

"Hey, when can I get the twenty dollars back I used to feed the kids?"

"Mama?" I asked, trying to figure out if it was a joke. "You are asking me about twenty dollars?" I didn't have the energy to argue or even go back and forth. I just assured her I would give it to her as soon as I could.

My heart shattered into a million pieces. As I laid on my death bed, she had the nerve to ask me about twenty dollars. She hadn't come to visit me in the hospital, nor had she asked how I was doing, but she was worried about twenty dollars. Not to mention, my girlfriend surprisingly stopped by my home the day of the incident around the same time my mother arrived. She heard the fire department complaining about how they had to constantly call her to see how far away she was. It took my mother an hour to get to my house when we only lived twenty minutes apart. My mother had the nerve to tell them she didn't leave the house any kind of way without getting dressed and putting on her makeup.

My real estate company that I had busted my butt to build, not only provided for my children and myself but for my mom as well. For the last five years, I had been assisting her with her bills, yet I was treated like a stepchild. I couldn't understand for the life of me what I did wrong as her daughter.

After that phone call, the doctor made everyone leave my room because my pressure went back up. They knew something was stressing me out, but they didn't know what. Had they heard the conversation I had with my mother, I'm sure they would have understood. I explained to the doctor that until I had my baby girl, my blood pressure would not stabilize. I needed my baby because she was only days old. The doctors agreed if it would fix my blood pressure. A good friend of mine was at the hospital that day, and I asked her if she wouldn't mind bringing my baby girl to me. She obliged.

When I held my baby girl in my hands after days of being away from her, it was like every bit of stress and frustration just melted away. Doctors were amazed that all that time they couldn't get my blood pressure stabilized the moment I saw my baby girl, it went down. It was like she was my security blanket. She brought me peace in a hectic moment. I wanted to be better for her; I wanted to be healthy and alive for all my kids.

The hospital made accommodations for my baby to stay with me after seeing how my blood pressure improved. After a few days, I was released. Little did they know, my baby saved me. It felt good to be home. I was excited for things to go back to normal. Later, while at home, I heard voices telling me to throw my baby off the porch. I knew it wasn't right, but the voices assured me I would be doing the right thing, and everything would be better. I wasn't feeling like myself. It felt as if I was suffocating in a life jacket that was too small to save me. I felt worthless and started having suicidal thoughts. I called 911, and they rushed me to the hospital. Doctors told me I was suffering from postpartum depression, and it would usually go away after six months. They prescribed me medicine to help ease the emotional rollercoaster I was on and gave me some options for counseling.

It was a challenge at first. I was ashamed to talk to

someone. I was embarrassed to have those feelings as a mom, but it was good to know I wasn't alone. I had some good days in which I felt like super mom, and then there were days in which depression crept its ugly face back into my life only to tell me how much I sucked as a mom. It was helpful having someone to talk to and confirm I wasn't going crazy. My postpartum lasted off and on for about six months. I struggled, but I made it. I never took the meds because I wanted to continue to breastfeed. After six months, I no longer heard those voices, and light began to seep back in. After hiding from the world, I started to come back out and enjoy life. I began to do everything with the kids. The kids were exposed to so much over the last several months I felt like I had to do everything with them to make up time.

After I got over my depression, I focused on getting the weight off. I would do activities with the kids that would cause me to be active. We would go to the park, the mall, and places around the neighborhood that I could walk. One morning, after dropping the kids off to school, my baby and I went to the park. I was walking her around in her stroller when suddenly I became dizzy, and my body began feeling weak. There was no one around for me to signal for help, but before I fell out, I managed to call 911 from my cell phone. The next thing I knew, I was riding in an ambulance with my little girl crying for her mommy. Upon arriving at the hospital, doctors told me I wouldn't be leaving. However, my baby could stay with me.

"Listen, I can't stay. I have to get my children from school," I said.

"Ms. Harris, we can't let you leave. Please call someone and make arrangements for them to be picked up," the doctor said, sounding insensitive to my situation.

"Not again!" I cried. I thought that things were getting better. I called my neighbor and informed her of what took place. I asked if she could pick the children up from school because the doctors refused to let me leave.

"Sure, you know I got you. What did the doctor's say was wrong with you?" she asked.

"I don't know. They won't tell me," I whined.

"Okay, no worries. I will get them. You just get better."

It was a relief knowing that my kids would be taken care of. I tried to relax, but I still wasn't sure what was going on with me. Honestly, I didn't think the doctor did either. About an hour later, my neighbor called me from my daughter's school.

"Hey lady. They won't let me get your daughter. The principal is saying something happened that won't allow them to release her to me, nor will they tell me why," my neighbor explained.

"Put the principal on the phone," I stated. Confused and frustrated with what was going on.

"Hi, Ms. Harris," said the principal sounding all nice.

"Hello, I'm currently in the hospital, and the

doctors will not let me leave. Please release my daughter to my friend."

"Well, something happened, and I don't know if it's a good time to tell you while you're in the hospital."

"Sir, we have no choice, or you will have to take my daughter home," I said, irritated at the moment. The principal takes a deep breath and sighs before choosing his next words.

"Your daughter had a suicide attempt today," he responded.

"No! My child would never do that," I yelled. "She doesn't want or need for anything. She has love and everything. There is no reason for her to do something like that." I assured him that he must have confused my child with someone else.

"Ms. Harris, we have proof, and she admitted it," he replied.

"God! Not my baby. No, not my baby. Help me, Lord, please help me," I screamed. My heart and chest felt heavy. *Everything I do is for my children. Why, Lord, why?*

The nurse came rushing in after she heard my scream.

"What's going on?" the nurse asked.

She grabbed the phone that hung from my hands.

"Hello?" asked the nurse as if she wasn't sure that someone would respond on the other end. I could tell the principal was still there as she gasped and covered her mouth in shock as to what she just heard.

I could hear the nurse through my cries, explaining

that I was in no condition to handle any bad news and that my blood pressure was abnormally high. A few beeps from the machine and the drop of the phone were the last things I heard before I passed out. My body couldn't handle the stress of the situation.

A few hours later, I woke up as if I had a bad nightmare.

"My kids. Where are my kids? I want my kids!" I shouted.

"Ma'am, calm down. They want you too. Your daughters are in the waiting area. However, we have to get you healthy for them," the nurse said, patting me on my shoulders as if that was going to appease me. That just infuriated me.

My blood pressure continued to rise. The doctors suggested that my kids come in the room with me in hopes that would calm me down. The girlfriend I asked to pick them up from school came in with the girls. I was grateful for her. She let me know that my son decided to stay at home with my sister, and everyone was okay. I held my children tight. I looked my oldest girl in her eyes and assured her that mommy loved her and never wanted to be without her.

Hours later, the doctors could tell that my blood pressure had stabilized. That was great news, but they kept me under observation for the next two days to ensure everything was okay. My daughters were right by my side and stayed in the hospital with me until I was released. The doctors warned me about my stress level and to be mindful of what I ate, or it could land me right back in the hospital.

I tried my best to alleviate stress from my life, but life still happened. As a single mom, I did my best, but my best landed me in the hospital five more times. Yet, each time no visit from my mom. Hurtful, I know, but don't feel bad. God had his reasons.

Shortly after my last visit to the hospital, I started planning to take my own life. I felt like things wouldn't get any better for me, so I took out a million-dollar life insurance policy to ensure my children would be taken care of. I went to my attorney and put a very detailed Will in place along with a trust account. I wanted to be selfish, not realizing the effect it would ultimately have on my children's life. I just wanted the pain to end, physically, emotionally, and however else it was there.

I had thoughts of walking in front of a bus. I thought about shooting myself and even overdosing. There were so many thoughts that went through my mind, and each day, I just couldn't stop thinking about how miserable my life was. With me being in and out of the hospital, I wasn't working as much, so funds were short. I felt awful as a mom, knowing that I couldn't provide for my kids, but God started showing up in the midst of my situation.

My investors allowed me to stay in the condo without paying any bills, and they provided money for me to feed my kids. I had an aunt, named Barbra, who had been trying to connect me with my sister on my dad's side for years, but my half-sister and I were stubborn, and we never made time. With me going through my situation and her going through a divorce, I figured why not, we both needed all the support we could get. She temporarily moved in with me to help out with the kids, even though she had her own home. We became close.

Without her help and support, along with my youngest daughter's godmother and my girlfriends, things would have turned out bad. It was as if God had heard all my complaints and was telling me that there was something to live for. Sometimes we can get so caught up in the moment and think God has forgotten about us, but God is so mindful of us.

I heard God say, "For being strong, I will provide an income that no amount of child support could replace." It was such a relief knowing that God was in the midst of my situation. It was like hearing his voice changed something inside of me. I got my health together and lost the majority of the weight. It took me three years to lose it all, but I did it.

I still ate what I wanted, but I did so in smaller portions. I stopped drinking sodas and only drank water. It was hard but doable. I found a trainer that pushed me yet was sensitive to my needs. He never gave up on me. I started going to the gym faithfully. With me working out and getting healthier, I fell out of depression and had a new outlook on life. I started taking back control and even started a new business. God has his way of using everything to bring him glory.

After my oldest daughter's suicide attempt, I

started to observe her, never letting her out of my site. During the process of coming out of my depression, I learned she suffered from an emotional support disorder, depression, and attention deficit hyperactivity disorder (ADHD). She was only nine years old when the symptoms started. After experiencing depression myself, I didn't want my daughter to ever go through what I went through. I sought out help for her, but even with professional guidance, she had a few more suicide attempts with one putting her in the hospital and another at a mental health hospital.

However, I refused to let the devil have my child. I prayed for her and all my children. I never wanted them to go through what I had experienced. After all that I had been through, I know the power of prayer, and I declared that the spirit of depression, mental turmoil, and everything associated with it was broken off our bloodline and declared emotional and spiritual healing.

I went from being sexually assaulted, involved in an abusive relationship, and broke and homelessness as a single mom to having a thriving business that supports my family. Over the years, I had my struggles that almost broke me, but I did more than survive, I thrived, and I have the scars to prove it. Today, I stand before you as a strong woman of God, CEO for an accounting firm, life insurance agency, and soon to be childcare center. I also own lots of assets and real estate. With all my success, I still chose to go to college to accomplish my degree. In an early chapter, I explained that God told me I would be more successful than I've ever been and would top the charts financially if I stayed the course and trust him. I did just that. These are the scars of my life, but they did not break me.

NOT BROKEN

As I stretched my arms and yawned from a good night's rest, I turned on my Sunday morning mix. I got up out of bed but as soon as my feet hit the floor, the rhythm of the music and the voices of praise moved my body. Before I knew it, I was dancing to my favorite church songs, and I opened my bedroom door so the music could carry throughout the house.

"Wake up!" I shouted down the hallway. Dancing all the way to my son's bedroom, I knocked and then opened his door. "Son, it's time to wake up and get ready for church."

"A few more minutes, mom," he groaned as I pulled back the sheets on his bed.

I smiled and danced my way to my oldest daughter's bedroom.

"Wake up!" I sang.

"It's too early, mom."

"We got to go, sweetie."

Her inquisitiveness made her jolt up out of bed. "Where are we going?"

"Church. Any more questions, ma'am?"

"I mean, we're always going to church–but I've never seen you this happy."

"Well, today I am feeling good. Ain't God good? Now, help me get your baby sister dressed."

"Ok," she complied, wiping the sleep out of her eyes.

Today was different. I woke up with so much joy and happiness that I couldn't contain it. All I could do was worship and dance! It was such consuming feeling inside of me.

We arrived at church in enough time to get some good seats up front. The choir ministered to my soul, causing tears to flow like a river. Every song made me realize how strong I was and how I had survived it all. Through the heartache, the abuse, being broke and not knowing what to do, losing my mind...through it all, God was there. God loved me through my foolishness. He loved me when I wasn't doing right. He never forsook me. He was there all along.

While the choir was singing, it felt like something was breaking off of me when I realized that I didn't have to be a victim. Part of me was ashamed and prideful at having gone through all the things I went through, but I knew I no longer had anything to be ashamed of.

When the pastor took over and started preaching, I felt like he was speaking directly to me. It was as if he was reading my mind! At the end of his sermon, I stood up and cried my heart to God. I felt my heart overflowing with the love of God as I prayed for mercy over my children and me. Women began to gather around me, pointing their hands in my direction and praying with me.

As I worshipped, one woman held my hand and begin to pray. As she prayed, I felt the glory of God come over me. After blaming God for all that I had gone through, I had accepted the role I played. I had to forgive myself. I was so ashamed for blaming God for my mistakes and my failures all this time, that I asked God to forgive me. I told her that I wanted to rededicate my life to Christ. As she prayed the prayer of salvation, the women around me began to celebrate. The Bible states that angels rejoice when someone gives their life to Christ! We praised God that day.

I had been fascinated with the industry men I was dating, caught up in the money and fame. I had the house, the money, the cars, I hung out with celebrities, and I really thought nothing could go wrong, as if I was living in some fairy tale. I was full of pride, but God stripped it all away. I was putting material things and people before him.

But pride and yielding to my will instead of God's will led to my downfall. My life had been spiraling out of control, and I was trying to find my way out. The world glorifies doing things that please your flesh because it feels good. We see it in movies, television, social media, and everywhere we look. The devices and schemes of the enemy are all around. But when you are caught up in feeling good and think that you have things under control, that's when the enemy takes you on a rollercoaster ride from hell.

But I thank God that He heard my cry and gave me grace! I had to humble myself before Him. The moment I submitted my will to God is the moment I was able to regain my focus and rebuild my spiritual life...the devil no longer had a chance! I made up in my mind that "no weapon formed against me shall prosper."

I broke the generational curses that had been in my family for years: mothers not knowing how to love their children, no one having true success. After church service that day, I felt free and full of life. I was so full of joy, I just wanted everyone to feel the way I did...I wanted everyone to experience the goodness of God like I had! We went home and I prepared a big meal for the kids and myself: barbecue Cornish hens, home-made mac-n-cheese, collard greens, and cornbread. I threw down! I couldn't help but smile for the rest of the day. The kids thought I had completely lost my mind. But what they didn't know is after years of being lost, their mother had become a new person in Christ.

I felt like a new me deserved a new beginning, so I rebranded my business and went back to school to finish my business degree. I've continued to thrive and since then I've opened my own property management company, an accounting firm, became an insurance broker, started a consulting firm, became a motivational speaker, and I am currently working on launching a childcare center. Now, I can add an author to the list! I have been able to do all of that *and* be a mother, all because of God's grace.

God wants what's best for each and every one of us, but many times we have distractions, people, and idols that we put before Him. Reflect on your life to see if there is anything you are putting before God. God taught me it's okay to have nice things; however, don't worship them. I honor the Blessing-Giver and not the blessings.

A lot of times we can think it's other people, but sometimes it's really us. I needed to take time out to analyze myself and ask, "Why did I choose these types of women and men to be around? Why does this always happen to me?" I needed to figure out why I made the choices I made.

It's important to get in tune with where God has you. What God has for you is for you, so stop worrying about everyone else. Figure *you* out. Maybe you have a jealous spirit, which is why God hasn't blessed you. He's showing you that you have to become a better you before He can give you the desires of your heart.

One of my desires was to experience healing within my family. Despite my mommy issues growing up, my relationship with my mother has matured, and we are becoming better with our communication. I'm also currently in the process of helping her get her first home. I have slowly started reconnecting with my sister, whom I hadn't spoken to in years. Growing up, I was hurt and one thing I've learned is that, "hurt people, hurt people." We are to hold people accountable for their actions but forgive them. We don't know what a person has been through or what caused them to behave in such a manner. Coming to that realization has really helped me on my healing journey with my family.

No one is perfect, and we all have battle scars. There are women who are going through what I went through and need to hear my story. They need to know that not all is lost, and they are worthy. What you've been through isn't who you are, it's only building you up for the amazing woman you are becoming. I am no longer a victim, I am victorious. I have a new perspective on things, and my outlook on life has changed.

I stand before you, scarred all over, but not broken! My past relationships did a number on me, but guess what? I'm ready to be loved and ready to give love. Hindsight is twenty-twenty. Before, I thought I was ready, but I really wasn't. God has worked on me throughout this journey. The man that gets to be with me now will have the best version of me because I have allowed God to make me over.

I leave with this. It's okay to support a scarred person, whether it be a friend or a relationship...but one thing you *can't* do is fix a broken person. It will be impossible! It is not your job to fix someone who is broken. Only God can make someone whole.

I pray and hope that my testimony has helped you. If you are going through a storm or are trying to heal from your scars, it's not too late to dedicate your life to Christ. Watch how He changes things around!

-Catrise.

ABOUT THE AUTHOR

Catrise Harris, born Laquilla Catrise Harris, is a survivor that owns an accounting firm, insurance company, consulting firm, and soon to be childcare center. Life has not always been like this for her. She has struggled throughout her childhood and young adult years. Through it all, she has come out stronger and better. Catrise is working on her second degree in Business Management with a certificate in Entrepreneurship.

She resides in Georgia with her three beautiful children whom she enjoys spending her time with. In addition to being with her children, she enjoys comedy for laughter and music to feed her soul. Despite the adversities that she has faced in her earlier years, she has learned to rely on her belief in God and the love from her children to get her through.